AF479069

JOAN WATTS

JOAN WATTS

Louis Grachos

Lilly Wei

RADIUS BOOKS SANTA FE

One's work is nothing but the long journey through life to recover, through the detours of art, the two or three great and simple images that first gained access to one's heart. Often, one has no choice but to make this journey—for good art is about necessity—the need to understand and express ourselves. And, as a bonus, we may in the process discover more of who we are.

— ALBERT CAMUS

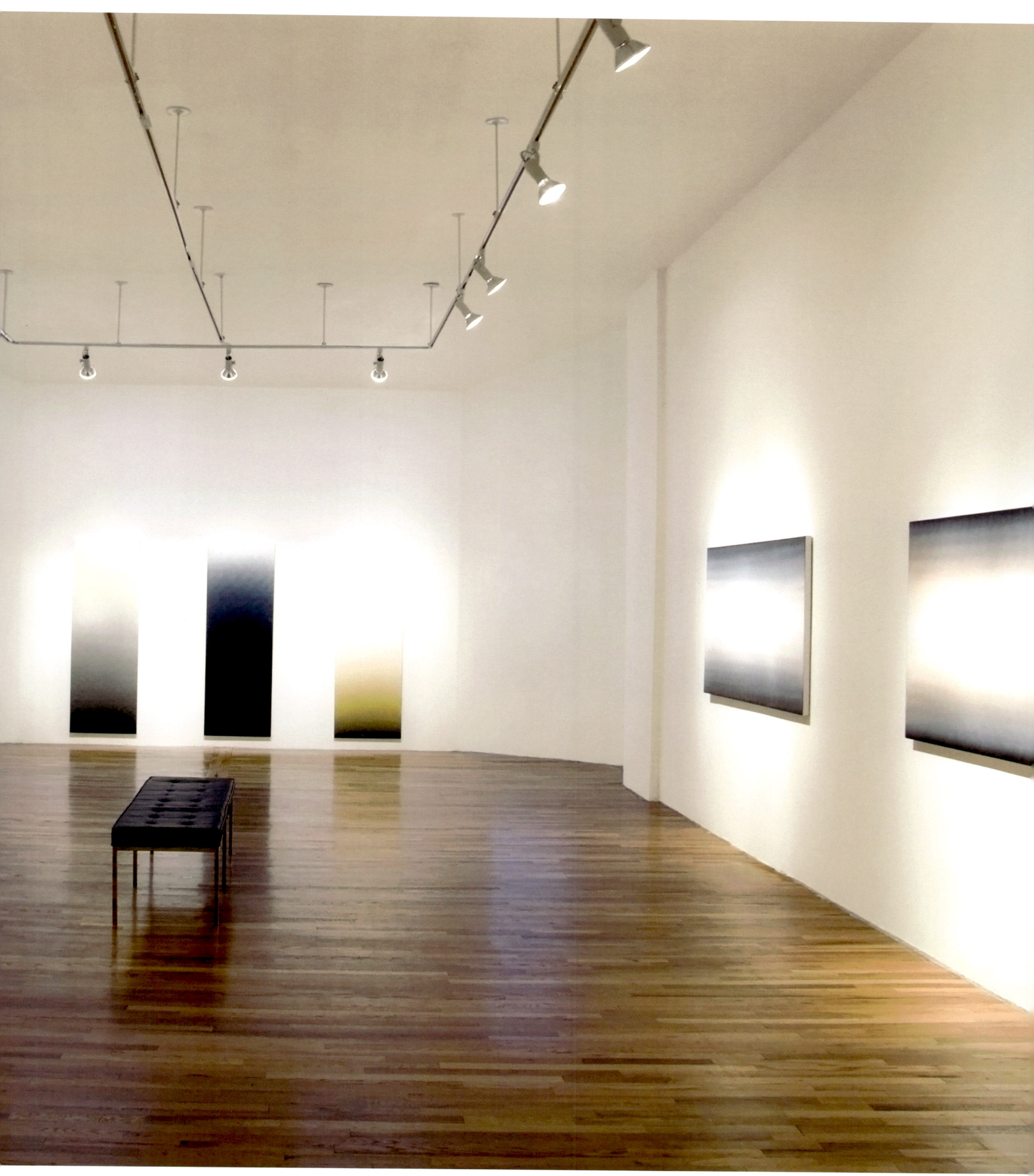

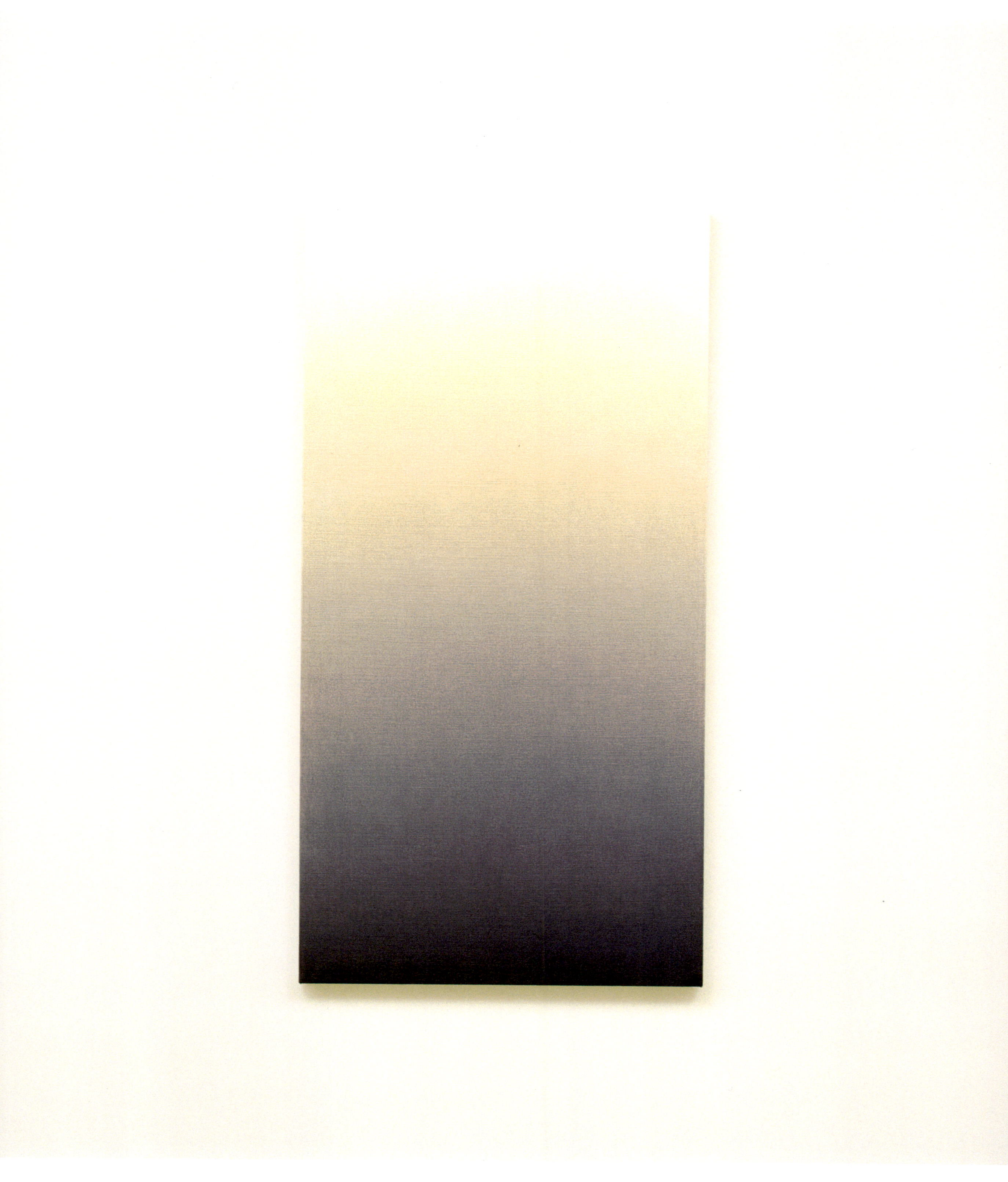

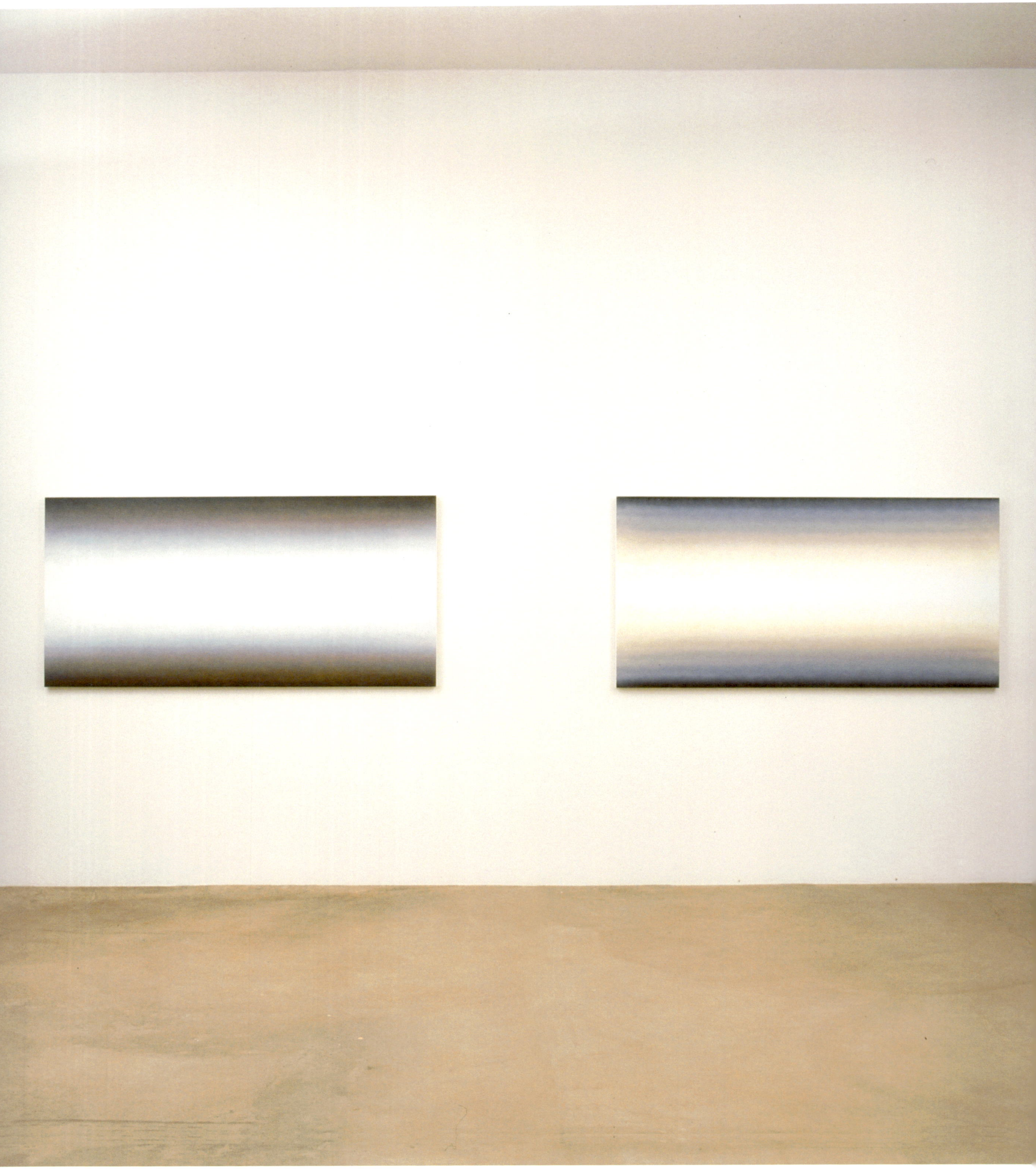

Contents

Foreword

Louis Grachos
Director, Albright-Knox Art Gallery

left: Installation View
detail from *White Series*, 2000

I FIRST MET THE PAINTER JOAN WATTS on a visit to her Santa Fe studio in 2000. Hanging on the walls of her pristine, light-filled studio was a series of twelve-inch square perfectly placed white canvases. The effect was mesmerizing. Each canvas filled the viewer's perceptual space and, at the same time, defined a cerebral zone for contemplation. The delicately nuanced surfaces of these paintings are evidence of an artist whose subject matter is light and whose understanding of translating both light and space into the simple format of paint on canvas was profound.

Joan Watts has never been swayed by the trends of the art market and while her early works bear a superficial resemblance to those of Robert Ryman and other Minimalist painters of the 1970s, she does not share their concerns with the essential nature of painting. Rather, her intent is more closely allied with the atmospheric wall divide installations of James Turrell, the meditative grid paintings of Agnes Martin, and Robert Irwin's scrim and light works. Turrell and Martin share Watts' love of the light and landscape of the American West, and the process of translating those elements into a work of art. Like Robert Irwin, Watts attempts to capture the ephemeral qualities of light and perception—not in three dimensions, but in the two dimensions of a painting's surface.

Since 2000, Watts' career has been devoted to fine-tuning her focus. Her newest series builds upon the experiments and explorations of her career, but also represents an important next step. These canvases are infused with brilliant color, which is a marked departure, and are characterized by an acute subtlety and refinement of technique. It is undeniable that the environment and the light of the New Mexico landscape now emanate from every work.

Watts' career-spanning obsession with capturing these effects of light is so evident in this more recent work (see *Series X* and *Channel Series*, pages 250–283). The natural tones and delicate surfaces she

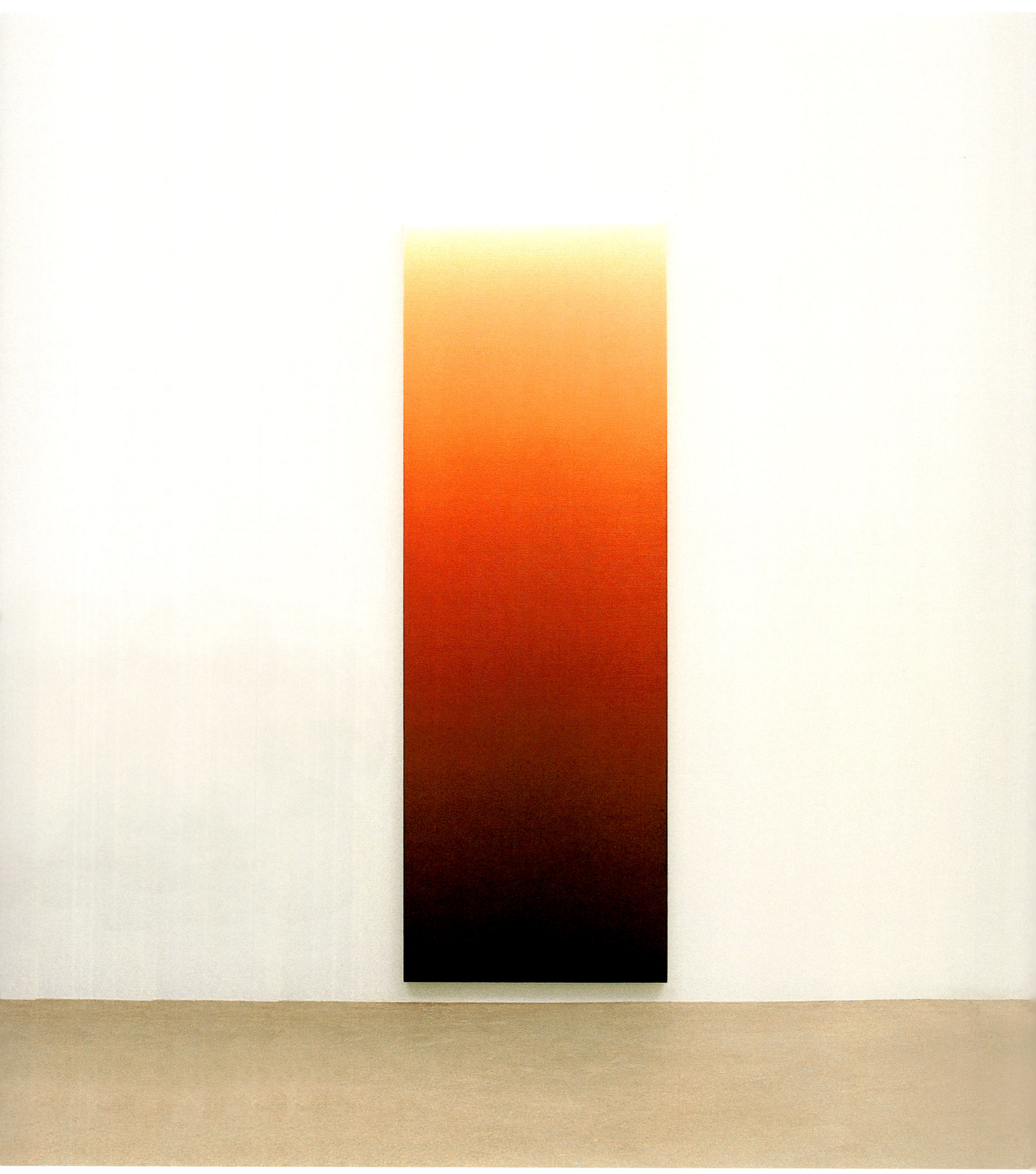

left: *III-3*, 2004

creates remain concentrated on portraying the essential qualities of light. Larger in scale than those works I first experienced in her studio seven years ago, these paintings address the viewer simultaneously on a cerebral and a physical level, since the dimensions and scale of these canvases reference the human body.

The remarkable 40-year development that this retrospective publication demonstrates—from the early mixed-media work to the current canvases—shows the careful progress of an extremely thoughtful and dedicated artist.

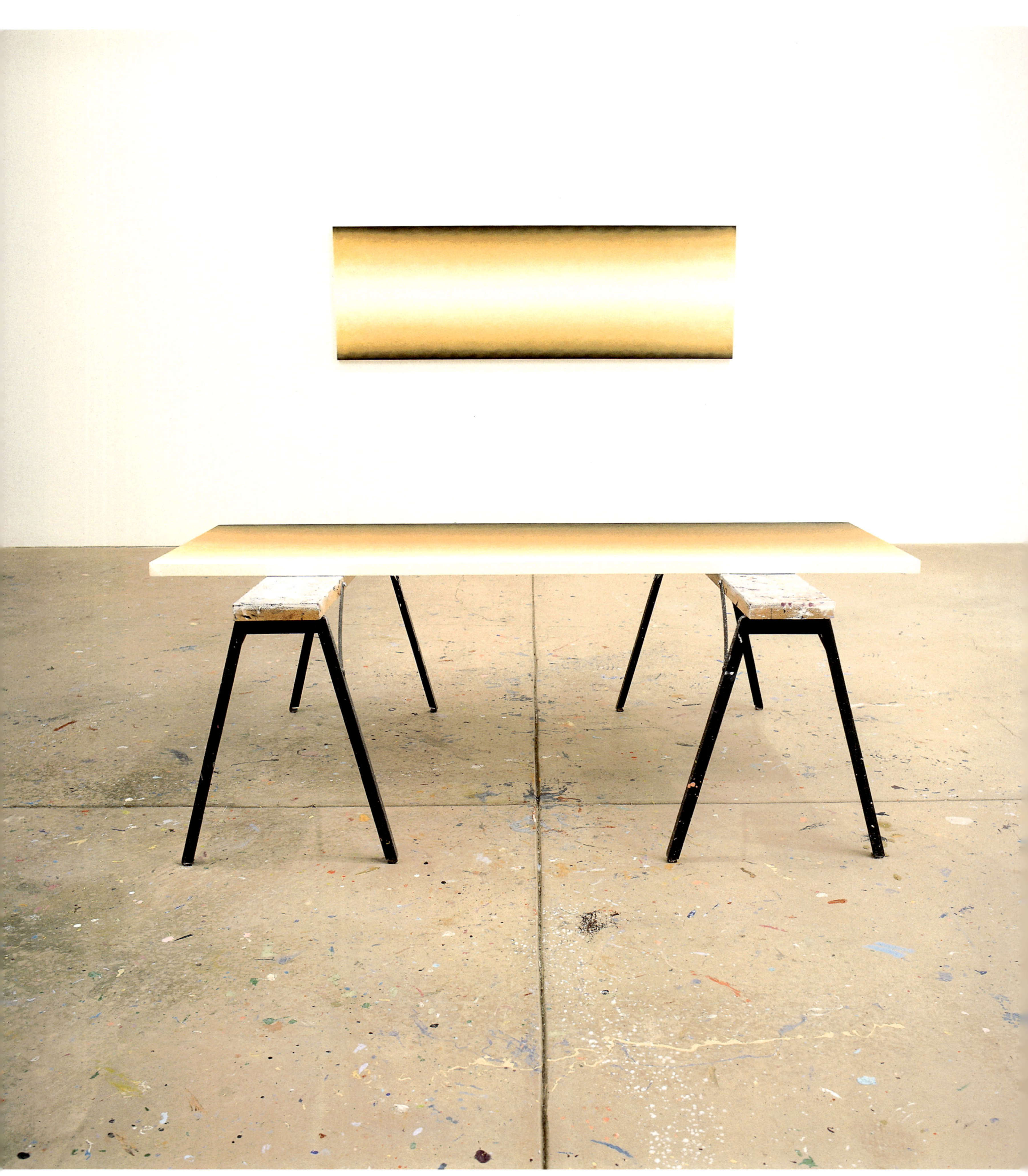

FIRST LIGHT: The Paintings of Joan Watts

Lilly Wei

left: Artist's studio, 2008
on back wall:
Channel 11, 2007

DURING A CONVERSATION THIS PAST JULY in her immaculate, light-filled studio with views of the Sangre de Cristo mountains, Joan Watts remarked, "I've been painting for 50 years and have not tired of it yet. That's the miracle."

Watts first became interested in painting when she was seventeen years old, but did not think of it as a serious endeavor in the beginning. She enrolled for two years as an art major at Briarcliff College, from 1957 to 1959, then went to Florence for six months, where she received private instruction while immersing herself in the masterpieces of that historic city. After Italy, she went to Florida, where she lived on the beach, enthralled by the flux of the weather, the play of light on water. It was then that she realized she wanted to paint, that painting was not merely a pastime but essential to her life. She enrolled at the San Francisco Art Institute in 1960 and earned her BFA in 1963. Going further west, she journeyed to Hawaii the next year to attend the University of Hawaii, receiving her MFA in 1966. She thought she would like to teach as well as make art and did so for more than twelve years before giving it up to concentrate uninterruptedly on her own work. In 1986, she moved to New Mexico and has been there ever since, living in the small town of Galisteo for ten years before moving to Santa Fe.

As she spoke, I thought about the quality of light in all the places she had lived and how that light had gradually seeped into her paintings until it filled them, the radiance welling up, spilling over. Light—created out of increasingly subtle modulations of color and contained within an imagined space, a virtual light trap—had become Watts' primary subject. It has been a quiet obsession, a gradual process of selection and paring down, culminating in a signature format that consists of variations on a finely calibrated field of oscillating color structured by a linear scaffold that is at times faint, at

FIG. 1 *Wheel* (detail), 1965, page 41

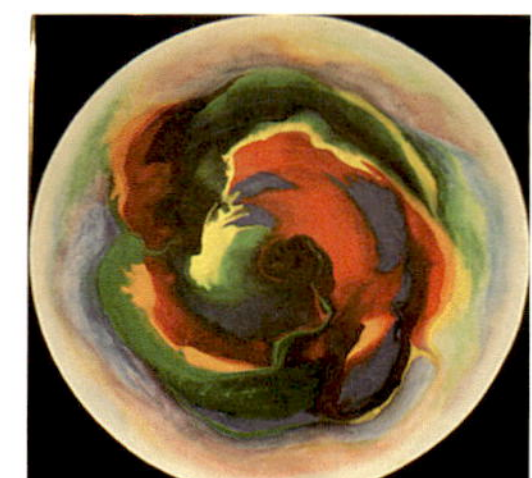

FIG. 2 *Circle in Square*, 1967

other times more pronounced. Although Watts' work is reductive, part of the modernist legacy and often considered minimalist, she insists it is not. Premised as it is on the immaterial and transcendent, in intention it has greater affinities to the paintings and statements of Agnes Martin, the installations of James Turrell and other artists of light and space, as well as to Buddhist teachings and the spiritual.

In 1965, while in Honolulu, Watts had her first breakthrough and began to make paintings that truly engaged her. She made them in series—a systematic but not programmatic process—that resembled an ongoing inquiry and suited her so well that she continues to use it. Watts painted circles inscribed in squares for four years, a motif that is not only modernist but also Classical and Renaissance, reflecting, perhaps, her stay in Florence and Italy. Her style was hard-edged, geometric, and boldly colored. Centered in each circle was a symbol that was also hard-edged and geometric—a Maltese cross, a Star of David, a Dharma wheel—that over time changed into more personal, biomorphic emblems (Fig 1). As she neared the end of this sequence, Watts was applying cut-out shapes to the canvases, and her medium changed from oil to a mixture of oil and acrylic. Unfortunately, this first group was destroyed en route from Hawaii to New York, but they had been photographed and the documentation remains.

Watts began another circle and square series in 1966 in New Paltz, New York (Fig 2), soon after joining the faculty of the State University of New York. She eliminated oil paint altogether, switching to acrylic and stretching the diameter of her circle larger—to 48 inches. She experimented with pouring, keeping the paint within the confines of the circle and savored the freedom of the process, as the paint made its own patterns, which evoked moonscapes and other cosmic topographies.

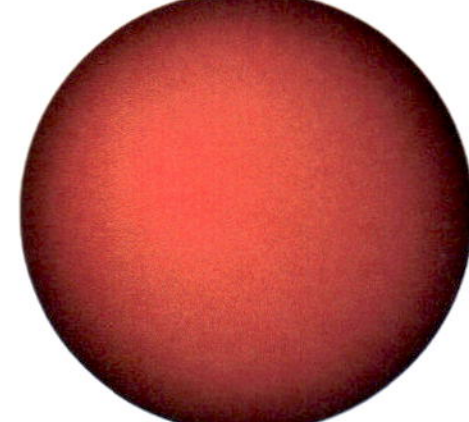

FIG. 3 *Tondo 34*, 1971, page 73

The circle was a resonant image for Watts and her response to it was spontaneous and deeply felt. In the end, it engrossed her for a total of seventeen years. While Watts did not adopt it for its symbolism, at least not consciously, she was certainly aware of its wide-ranging metaphoric and iconographical implications. Associated with fullness, harmony, and perfection, the circle simultaneously represents emptiness and nothingness—opposites that constitute a completeness. It is macroscopic—an emblem of the world and the cosmos—and intimate, an age-old symbol of female sexuality and fecundity. It also represents her personal trajectory, which tends to be circular. Her beginning will most likely be her end, but this is not to say the paintings are the same, merely that Watts, like Mondrian, Ad Reinhardt, Agnes Martin, and Robert Ryman, for instance, recognizes that repeating her chosen tropes will always yield new discoveries, new works.

In 1969, Watts eliminated the square, freeing the circle from its frame. She thought of these tondi as monochromatic or tonal color-field paintings (Fig 3). Then she retired the circle motif, thinking she had exhausted it. It turned out she had not, returning to it five years later, in 1974.

In the interim, she became intrigued by process art. She started pouring polyurethane onto unrolled plastic sheets and dropped powdered pigment onto it. The reaction sealed the pigment into the plastic, resulting in paintings that almost made themselves. Watts found this exhilarating for a while but soon tired of it. Chance as the fabricator was not challenging enough for her temperament. Also, the materials were extremely toxic, though few artists at the time (one thinks of Eva Hesse and Nancy Graves) paid enough attention to the dangers of their métier or safeguarded themselves adequately.

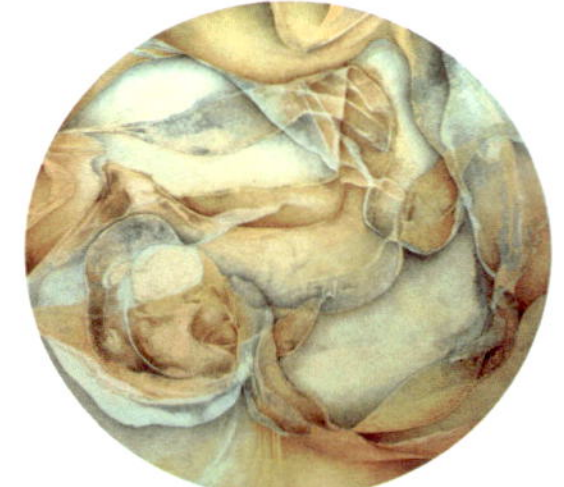

FIG. 4 *Circle 41*, 1978, page 97

Watts then had the idea to substitute unrolled canvas for unrolled plastic. She covered the canvas with a layer of cheesecloth, using rhoplex as the adhesive because it dried transparently. Over this, she poured earth-colored acrylics and a few other colors. She also stained the crumpled, textured surfaces, which were hung without stretchers, like hanging Asian scrolls. This series she found more satisfying because she had more control over the finished paintings. It also led her back to the circle. She became curious about the shape again, which she still found compelling, armed with these new methods and materials. Using yards of cheesecloth which she layered, Watts walked around the 48-inch and 60-inch circular canvases in a kind of ritual circumambulation, draping them with the gauzy fabric. She then covered the surface unevenly with rhoplex. During the long drying process, she adjusted and readjusted the folds of the cheesecloth until she was satisfied with the arrangement. Afterward, she poured acrylic over the gauze, stained it with sponges, then hung the tondo on the wall and painted sections of the surface with a brush for further definition. The paint and crushed cheesecloth merged into each other and the whole had a rhythmic, often spiraling movement that strongly suggested natural phenomena: water rippled by wind; spindrift; cloud formations and dissolutions (Fig 4).

In 1978, a disastrous fire in her studio destroyed everything in it. She was devastated, but once again slides and photographs of the work, stored elsewhere, were saved. The fire was the catalyst for yet another move, another change. She left her teaching position and moved to New York, to SoHo—then in its heyday—where she rented a loft. It was time to start again. She continued to make her poured and painted tondi, extending their diameter to 72 inches and making the colors more vivid, increasingly luminous, the centers smoothed,

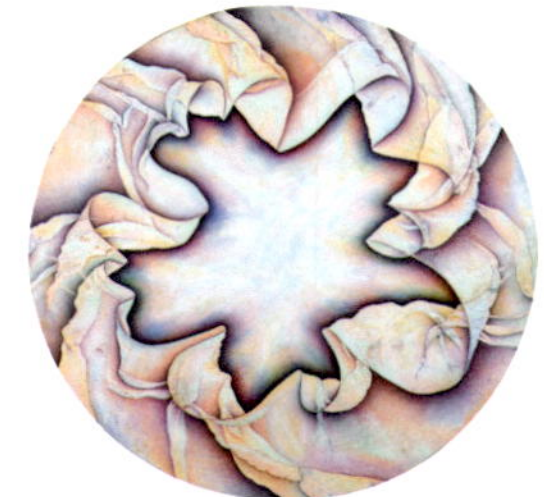

FIG. 5 *Circle of Light*, 1983, page 111

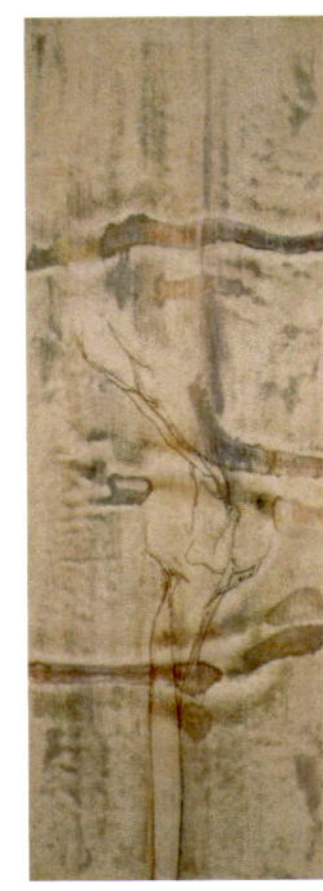

FIG. 6 *Wall Hanging 40*, 1982, page 123

without visible brushwork. These appealing works suggested both an indeterminate cosmic space as well as an abstraction of the female sex. The gauze became a framing device, a threshold between the materiality of the fabric and the illusionism of paint, between the phenomenological and the spiritual (Fig 5).

Watts also returned to the unstretched scrolls she had made previously, scaling them to the human body (72 x 24 inches), although it was landscape they conjured up rather than the body (Fig 6). But she became restless, uncomfortable with the worldliness, artifice, and frenetic pace of urban living, stifled by the crowded streets, the noise and tall, illuminated buildings that blocked the sky and dimmed the stars. She decided to change her life once again.

Watts moved to New Mexico and has lived there now for more than twenty years. Visiting the area often with her parents in her childhood and returning many times in later years, she was always dazzled by the light, the breathtaking vistas and boundless skies of the Southwest. She was so awed by living in her new surroundings that she did not paint for a year, as she acclimated and built herself a house and studio in Galisteo. Although she had brought an ample supply of circular stretchers with her from New York, she never made another tondo. Instead, when she began to paint again, she painted landscapes. How could she not? she asked. "Never before," she wrote in a brief overview of her life as a painter, "had I experienced so intimately and so fully the impact of land and sky, dawn and dusk." In that ancient, uncompromised domain of high deserts, plains, mountains, cacti, juniper, tumbleweed, of stillness, silence, solitude, and the immensities of space, the conditionality and transience of human existence must be keenly felt.

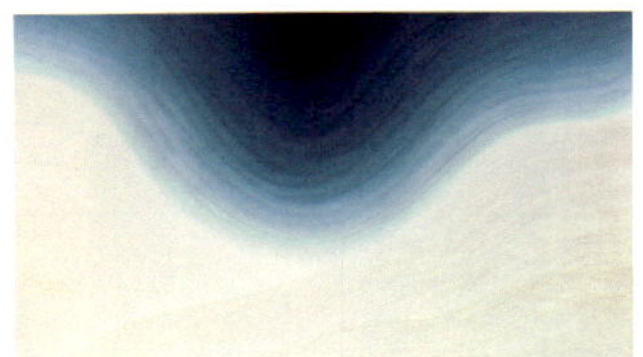

FIG. 7 *White Sands*, 1988, page 147

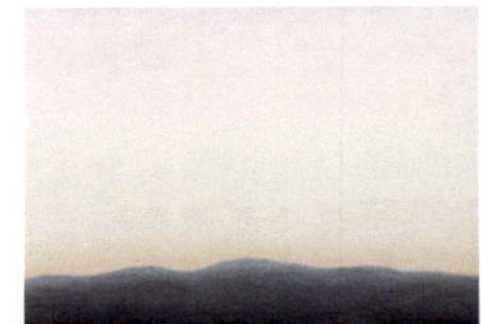

FIG. 8 *Early Morning Light*, 1987, page 129

Watts approached the landscape tentatively at first, mimetically, but soon her paintings became more reductive, simplifying forms in paintings such as *White Sands* (1988) (Fig 7) and *First Light II* (1988) (page 137). She contrasted the massive, uncanny shapes of the mountains with the emptiness of the sky and the shifting, crystalline light in a dialogue between the absolute and the ephemeral. These paintings were also built up in layers, the first clear acrylic applied directly by hand, to create texture and tooth. A layer of stained acrylic was added, succeeded by multiple layers of transparent oil glaze brushed and rubbed over the surface, the acrylic base still visible. The permeable surface permitted light to penetrate it and escape, reflected and refracted through many thin layers of transparent color for an effect of soft brilliance. In addition, Watts made a series of pastels—also layered—which were more improvisational and captured the tension between the passing moment and the permanence of the land with greater immediacy than the slow, carefully calculated paintings (Fig 8). Throughout the different stages of her development, she has made works on paper because she liked the directness of drawing or painting on surfaces other than canvas and because it permitted experimentation.

Transfixed by the entire region, Watts made three trips to southeastern Utah in the late 80s and early 90s which proved to be revelatory. The towering stone formations pierced by openings—the rock bridges, arches, and slot canyons—with their sharp demarcations of positive and negative space, solids and voids were important for her to see, inspiring the next series of paintings and works on paper. At this juncture, Watts rediscovered oil as a medium more suitable to the subtle tonalities of the light she was trying to depict.

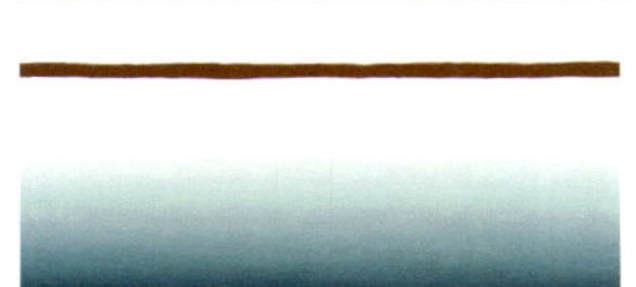

FIG. 9 *Two*, 1993, page 161

FIG. 10 *Yantra VI*, 1996, page 185

Watts was diagnosed with breast cancer in 1989 and once more altered her life in response. During her convalescence, she began to meditate, a practice that is now an integral part of her daily existence. She also redefined for herself the process of painting as a meditation in which the painting becomes the object of contemplation. She began to equate the exterior—the landscape that was pure light and infinite space—with the interior, which she said also depended upon "luminosity" and "spaciousness." As a consequence, her landscapes, with a band representing the earth that spanned the bottom edge of the canvas, no longer needed to be anchored. Set free, as a thick impasto line, it could float anywhere within the charged colored space of the canvas, since all phenomena could float in the meditative space, reconstituting the relationship of solid to void, of earth to luminous colored air, not as a division or duality but as a seamless, harmonious whole in constant transition **(Fig 9)**.

Watts' *Yantra* (visual meditation) series, begun in 1995, restored the square to her repertoire of forms, this time without the circle. These also contained geometric motifs but were blurred and softened, the structure almost imperceptible. Instead, a horizontal or vertical band, or sometimes both, crossed the modulated field of pale color as an aura, an emanation **(Fig 10)**. During this same time Watts painted a series called *Zazen* (meditation in paint). It evolved into a single, encompassing painting assembled from 26-inch squares installed in a linear sequence that extended 38 feet. Each of these paintings was divided in half, the bottom darker, the top lighter in a graduated scale that met in the middle as a bright, enigmatic band. As a sequence, they formed a long horizon line which represented the infinite vastness of the universe, the oneness of earth and sky. *Quartet (Channel I, II, III, IV)*, 2007, a group of four 24-inch squares, was similarly arranged and also

FIG. 11 *Beyond IXV*, 1999, page 203

bisected by a soft white line. *Hai-Ga* (painting haiku), 1999, was formed by a series of ten twelve-inch squares that extended nineteen feet. These small paintings were the palest of greys with a narrow, barely visible white line, as if the horizon were on the verge of vanishing and what remained was a glowing, immeasurable field of light.

Watts worked on a series called *Beyond* in 1988 and then again in 1999. Comprised of squares, the format was chosen for its neutrality, its lack of direction, its balance (Fig 11). When she began to paint landscapes on first arriving in New Mexico, she used a horizontal support, a conventional landscape format, especially for panoramic views. But soon afterward, she began searching for a much less representational solution. She wanted to paint a state of mind, a state of being, something more experiential and less traditional. These paintings were barely colored, the white tinged with the barest intimation of color to evoke clear, fragile light. Like the paintings in the series that preceded it, *Beyond* is characterized by a narrow median horizontal line, the whitest point of the painting, and the focus of it. Soon after, Watts gave up this division in her ongoing quest for simplification, unity, and clarity.

Watts frequently works with rags rather than brushes to make her delicately nuanced surfaces. Her canvases are first prepared with several layers of gesso. She then stains the surface in a repetitive application of oil paint, rubbing the color into the ground, then taking it away. As Watts builds up the surface, the paint becomes embedded into the canvas and lines begin to emerge. The weave of the canvas is picked up, which gives the surface its incidence and suggests a sensation of space, but without gestures or traces of the hand.

In 2000, Watts switched to a vertical format in a series called *Open*, executed in the same manner as *Beyond* and *Hai-Ga*. Nearly

FIG. 12 *0-11*, 2002

white, it is shadowed at the bottom and lighter as it ascends until it turns an almost pure white at the top, as if on an ultrasensitive rheostat, the movement as understated as the gentle inhalations and exhalations of breathing.

That autumn, Watts moved from Galisteo to Santa Fe. There, she designed and started to construct another house with a studio nearby. Intent on the project, she stopped painting for nearly a year for a second time, although she continually imagined the paintings she would make in this new location. Always attuned to her surroundings, she knew the move would precipitate a change in her work. The studio was completed first and she lived there while finishing the house. She wanted to return to color, and was excited by the vertical paintings she had been working on. This time, she used a 44 x 22-inch support, a 2:1 ratio, and began her *Zero* series, which, two years later, consisted of 40 paintings. *Zero*, or O, signified both void and completion, the nothing that is and the source of everything, the continuum. It also recalled her earlier tondi; now, though, it was not a shaped canvas but a symbolic title, a letter, number, and metaphor. For this grouping of elegant, splendidly hued, ever more luminous paintings—peach to rose to gold to azure along with warm and cool greys (Fig 12)—Watts chose a heavyweight canvas with a pronounced weave which she prepared by applying several coats of gesso brushed horizontally, which left traces of the brushstrokes. To this she applied layer after layer of color in her usual manner, wiping away the paint, which forced the color into the ground. Again, there was a gradual ascension, a surge from bottom to top, from the deepest, most vivid hues to the emptiness (or fullness) of white. What remained was more noumenal than physical as the light, created from the meticulously worked fluctuation of tones, rose upward, as if illuminated from within by a small rising sun.

FIG. 13 *X-13*, 2006, page 255

In the last few years, experimenting some more with formats, Watts pushed the dimensions to 72 x 24 inches, a 3:1 ratio that was the same as the hanging vertical scrolls of the late 1970s and early 1980s. Suite (2005) is a work that is composed of five of these paintings **(page 249)**. With a six-inch interval between each panel, it measures an expansive 144 inches in width in a ratio of 1:2. The sequencing is also graded from dark to light so the last painting is the lightest in the series.

Watts now began to scale the colors vertically as well as horizontally, from dark to light, (with black added) to be read from left to right within each painting **(Fig 13)**. Seeing the undulating patterns that appeared as she wiped away the paint, she incorporated them in the new work instead of erasing the marks. These "waves," created by the movement of her hand, disturbed the surface in a way that seemed "almost radical" to Watts after years spent eradicating the subjectivity of touch. Color was again muted and veiled but had also become more varied. At times, she turned the vertical into the horizontal and hung two panels side by side, lengthwise, as a diptych that extended to the edges of peripheral vision and beyond. These suggest seascapes, skyscapes, earthscapes, with their range of glowing nocturnal blues, oranges, reds, violets, yellows, greens—the entire spectrum—the shades lightening from left to right or from bottom to top. The colors are not quite the same as colors in nature. Watts has, from the beginning, infused the real with the sense of the abstract, the conceptual, or the reverse. They are pitched to sensation and the cessation of sensation, as the viewer is enveloped by their purposeful serenity, by their palpable color and light, ending in a blaze of almost pure white. This series she called *X*, "for the unknown."

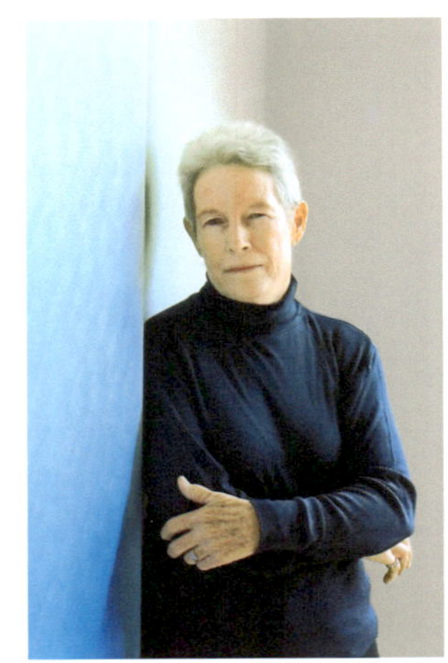

Watts in her studio, 2007, photo: Linda Montoya

Some of the newest work from 2006 is not so calm. Lurid, apocalyptic hues—black-red to blood orange to the flash of electrified yellow, the colors of a nuclear dawn or sunset, of a thermonuclear explosion—herald a change in mood once more, one that mirrors the volatile state of today's conflicted world, as she cycles within the self-imposed but endlessly variable limits of her repertoire.

Watts' elegant serializations—with their honed formal syntax that is surprisingly sensuous—function like a mantra of hypnotic, accumulating potency, each painting an invocation of sorts, a prayer. Watts has long been involved with Buddhism and it is to the condition of attentiveness or Buddhist mindfulness that she offers her practice. For her, painting is a way of life, an uncharted journey in which she relies greatly on intuition, an endeavor that she keeps apart from the more commercial necessities of the art world. Ultimately, in Watts' approach, painting is more fastidious and disinterested than that. It is matter-of-factly evidential yet connected to the spiritual, to creation myths and both the conscious and unconscious, to darkness that gives way to light and the tumbled forces of the universe. It depicts things seen and unseen and, at its best, is indisputably miraculous.

Plates

HARD EDGE SERIES

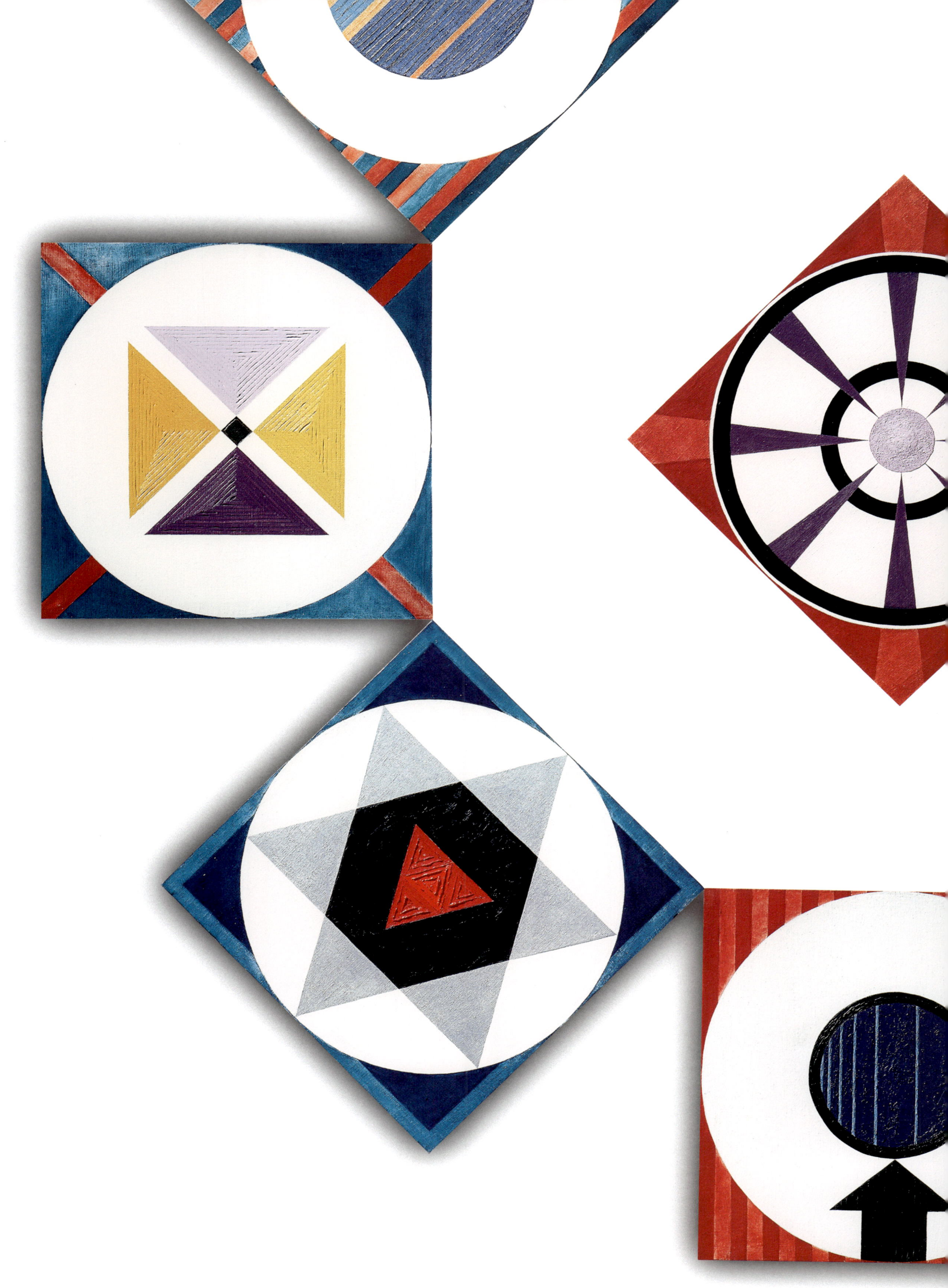

HARD EDGE SERIES

Wheel, 1965, oil on canvas, 78" x 78"

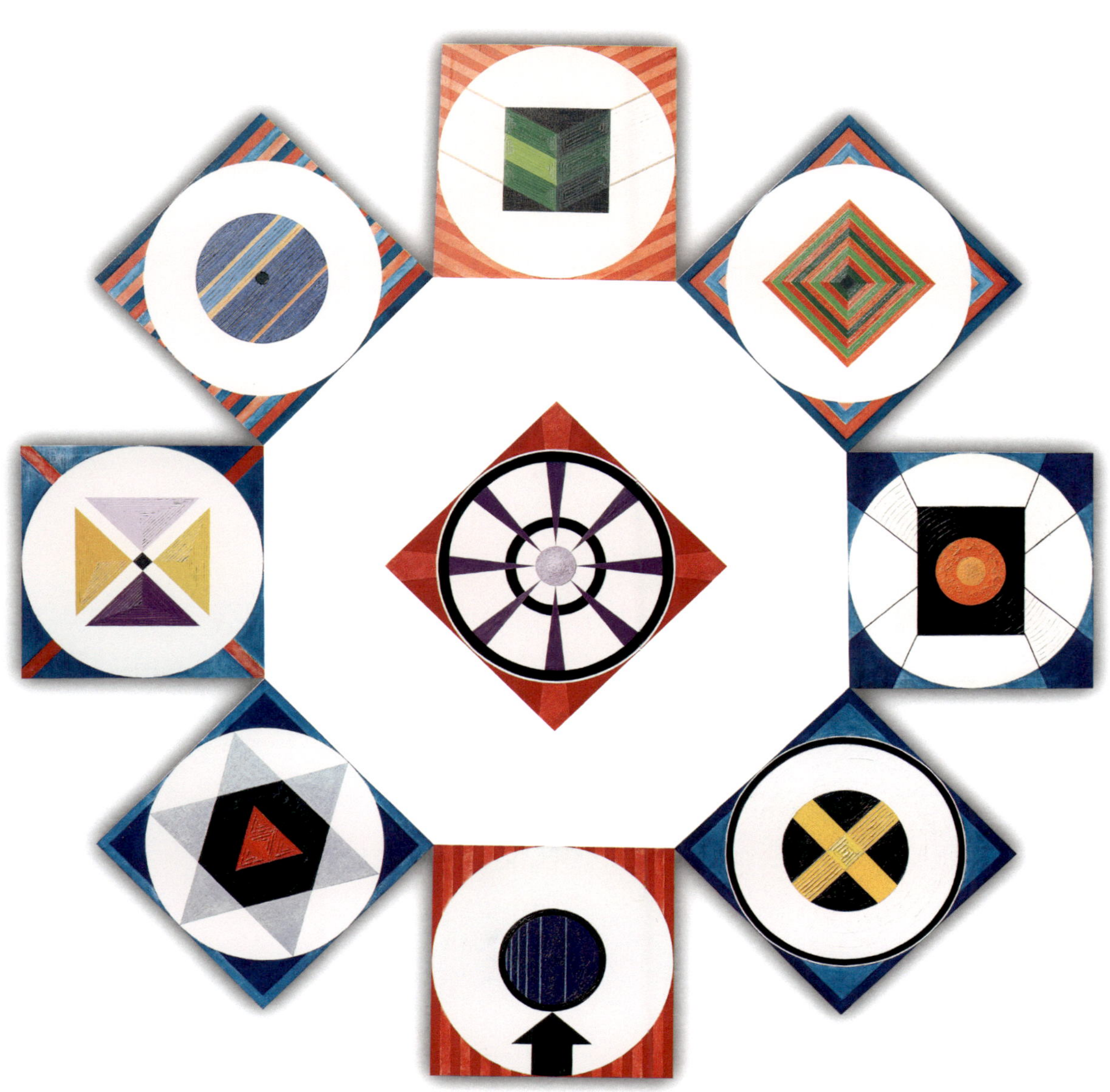

HARD EDGE SERIES

Wheel (detail), 1965, oil on canvas, 18" x 18"

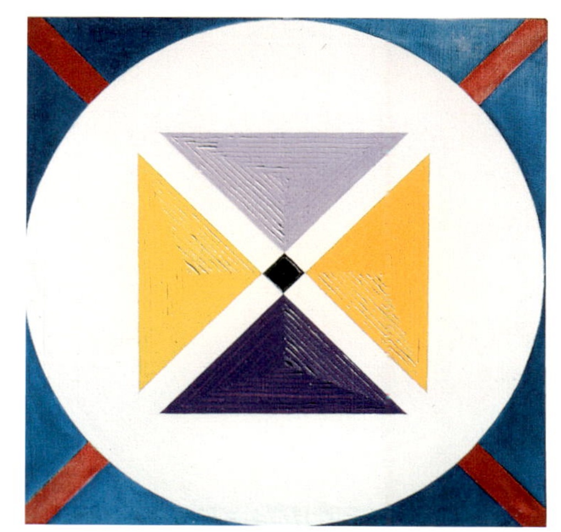

HARD EDGE SERIES

Wheel (detail), 1965, oil on canvas, 18" x 18"

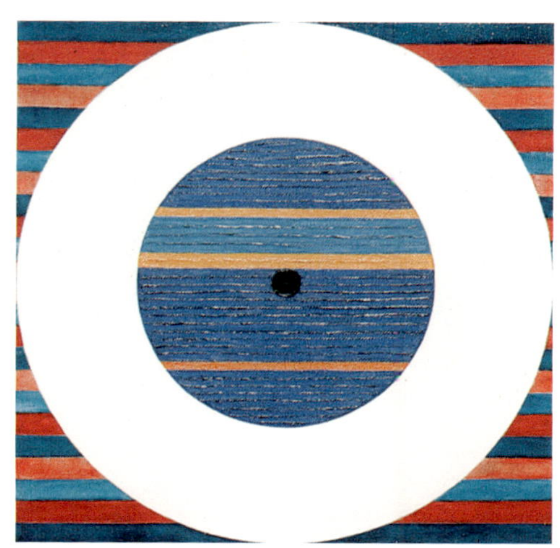

HARD EDGE SERIES

Wheel (detail), 1965, oil on canvas, 18" x 18"

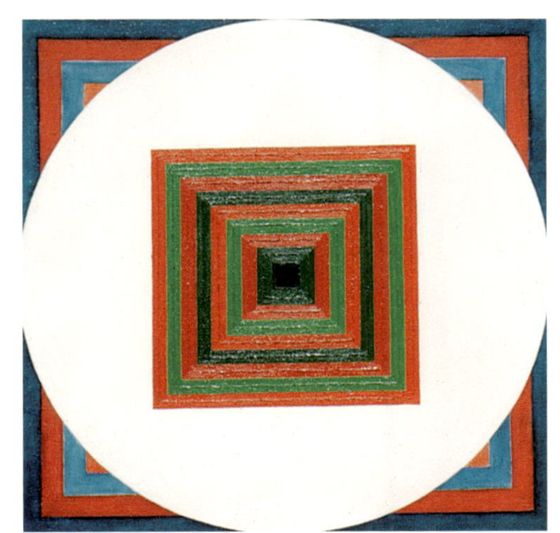

HARD EDGE SERIES

Flight, 1965, acrylic on canvas, 24" x 48"

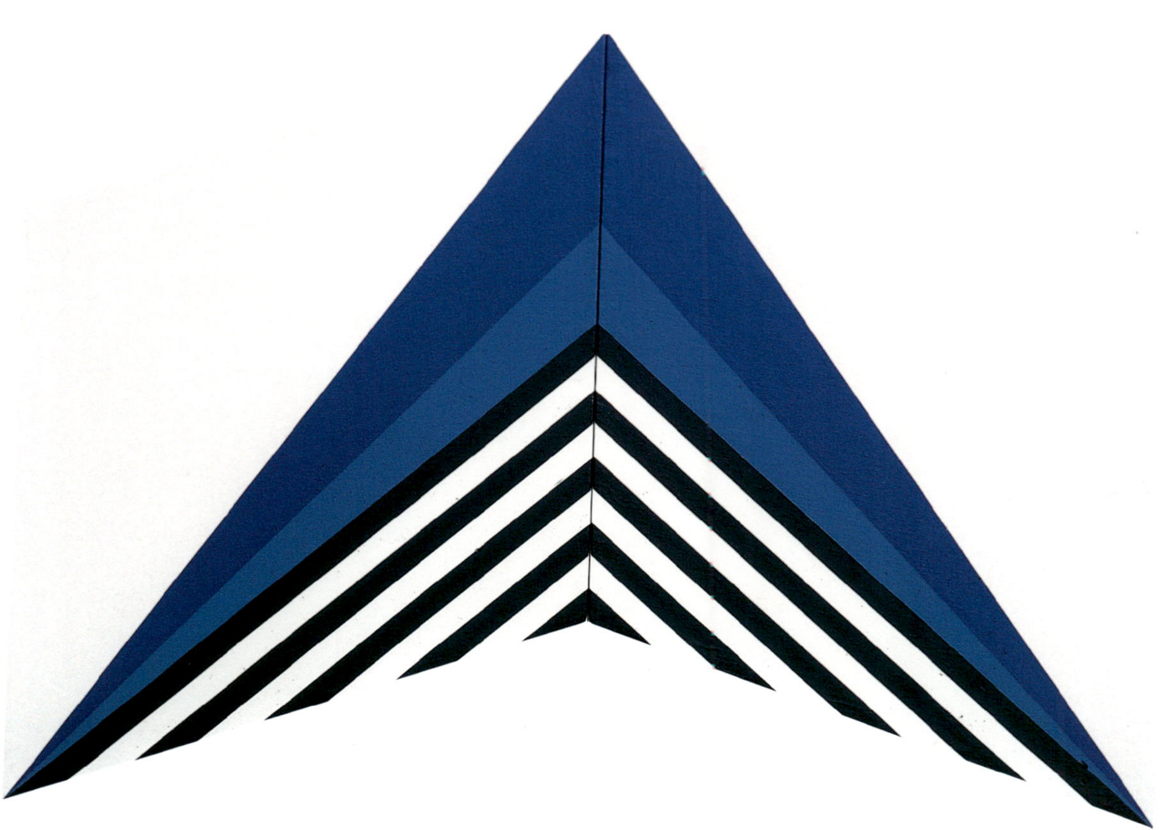

Icon 6, 1965, acrylic on paper on board, 6" x 6"

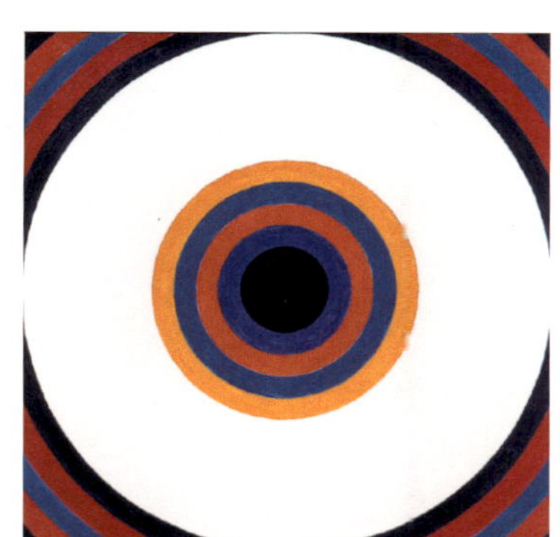

Icon 5, 1965, acrylic on paper on board, 6" x 6"

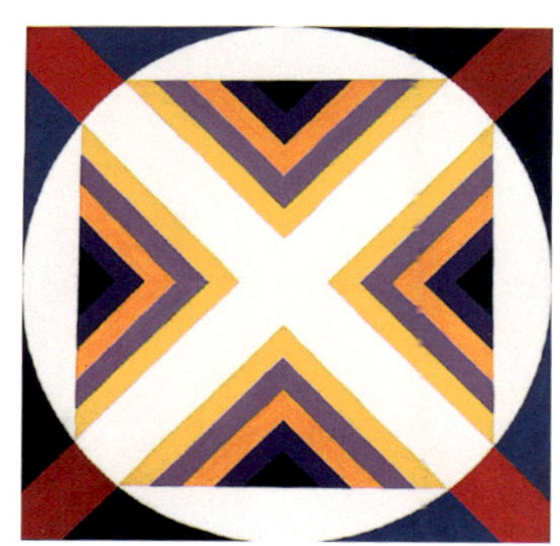

HARD EDGE SERIES

#11, 1966, oil and acrylic on canvas, 18" x 72"

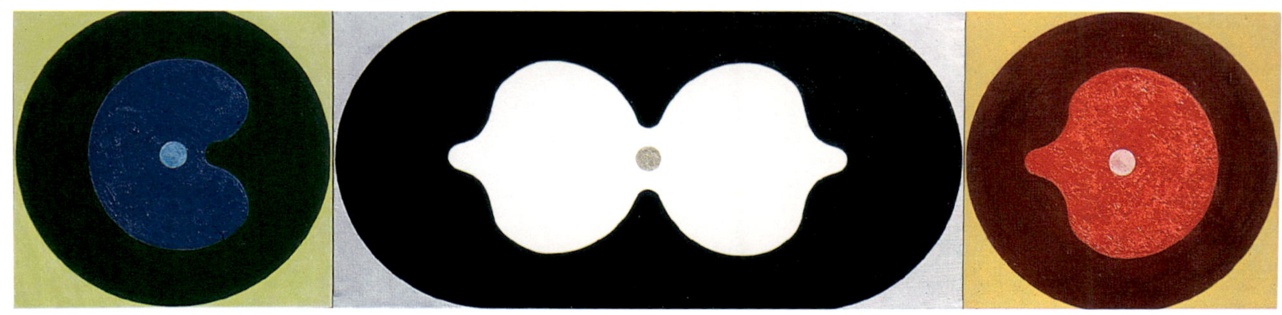

TONDO SERIES

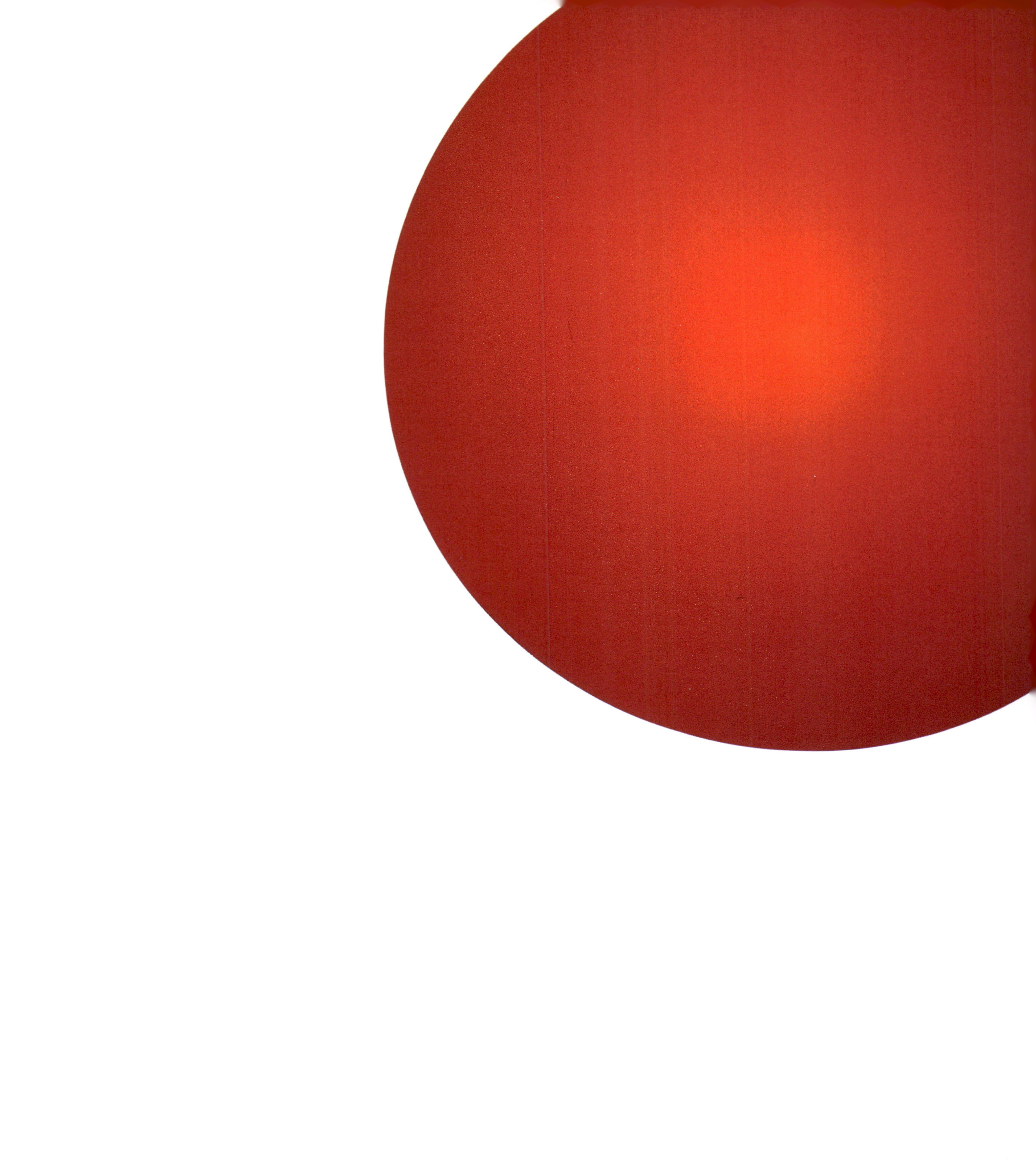

TONDO SERIES

Cloud, 1968, acrylic on canvas, 72" x 72"

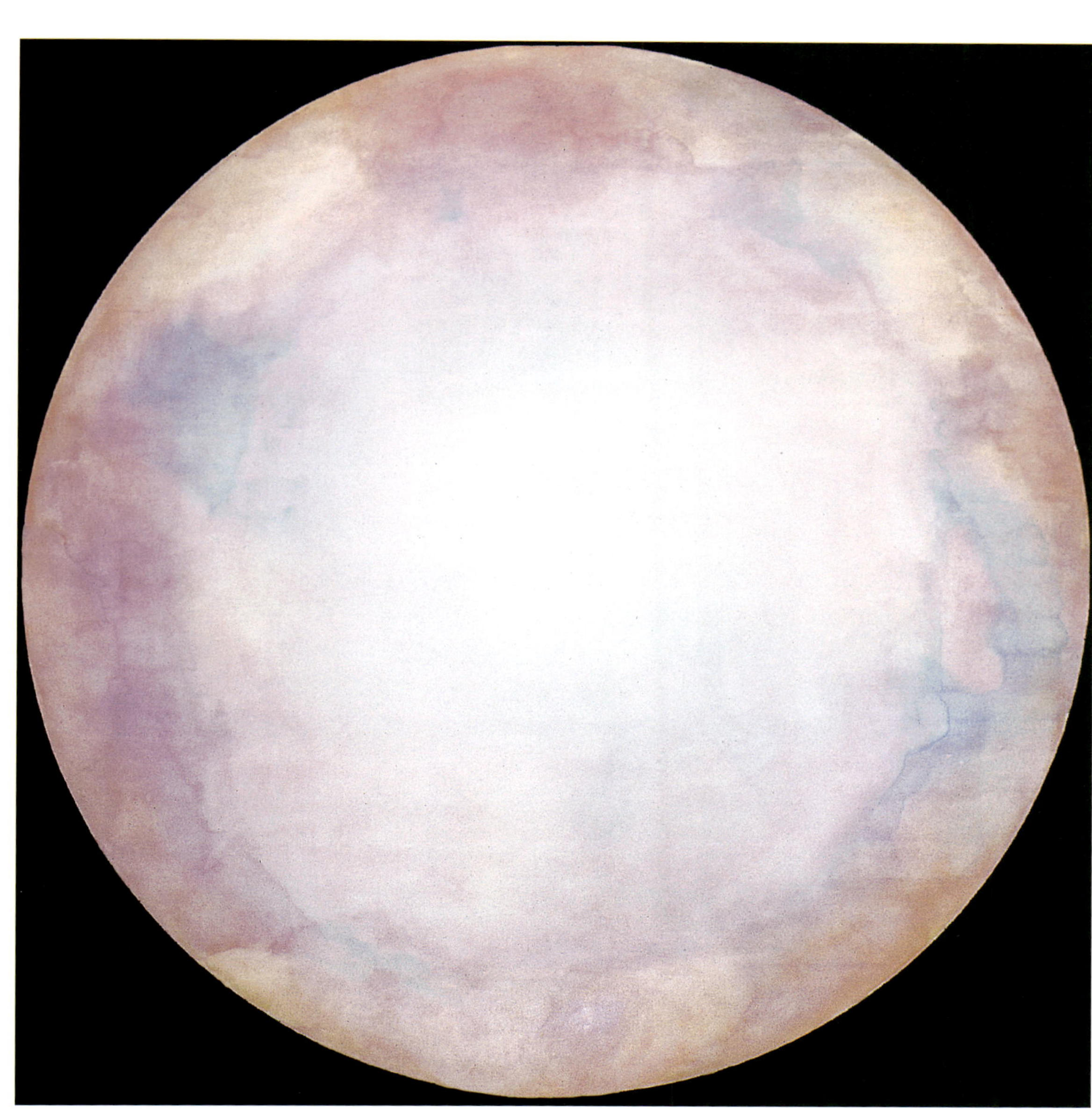

TONDO SERIES

Tondo 1, 1969, acrylic on canvas, 36" diameter

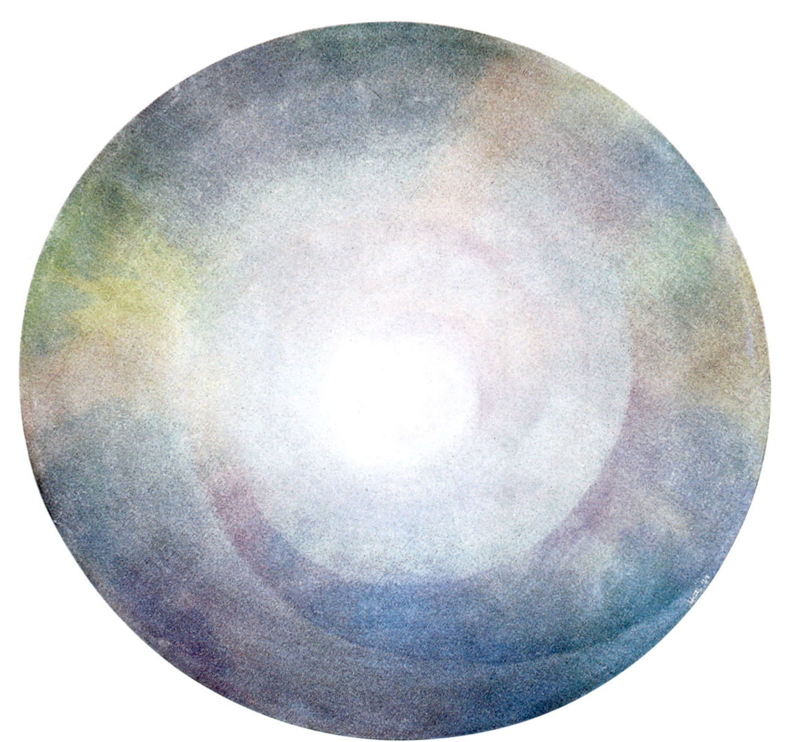

TONDO SERIES

Tondo 5, 1969, acrylic on canvas, 48" diameter

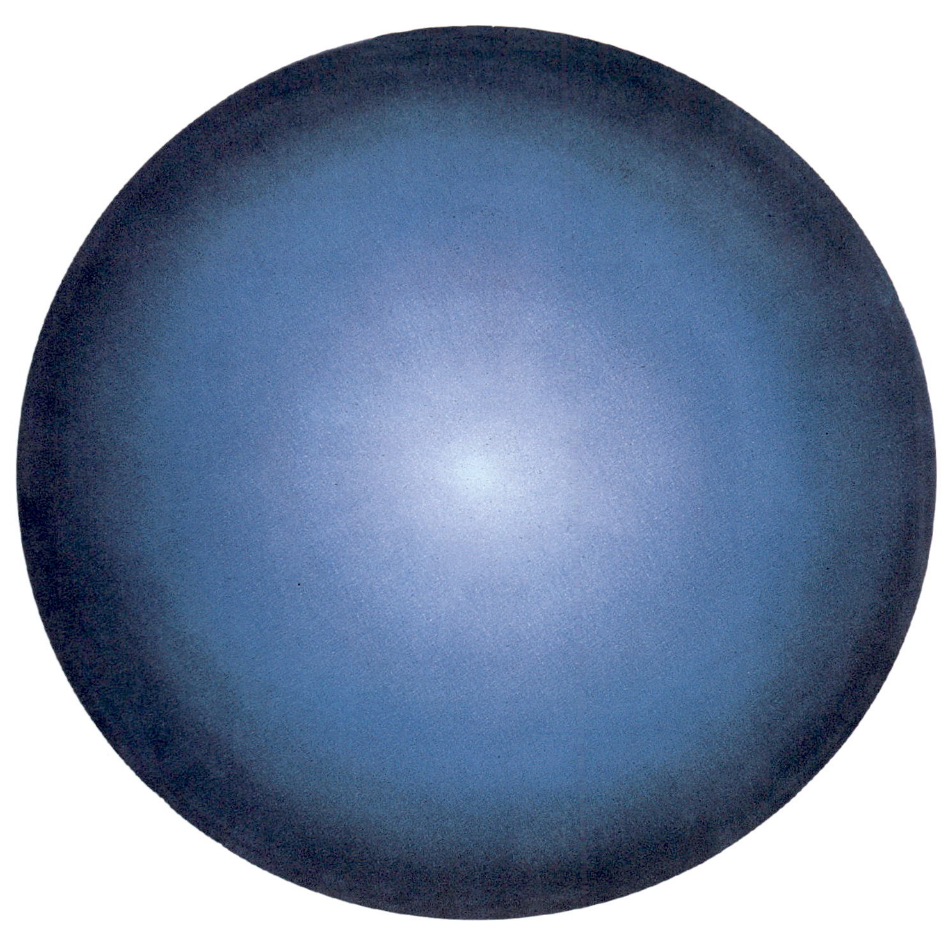

Tondo 8, 1969, acrylic on canvas, 36" diameter

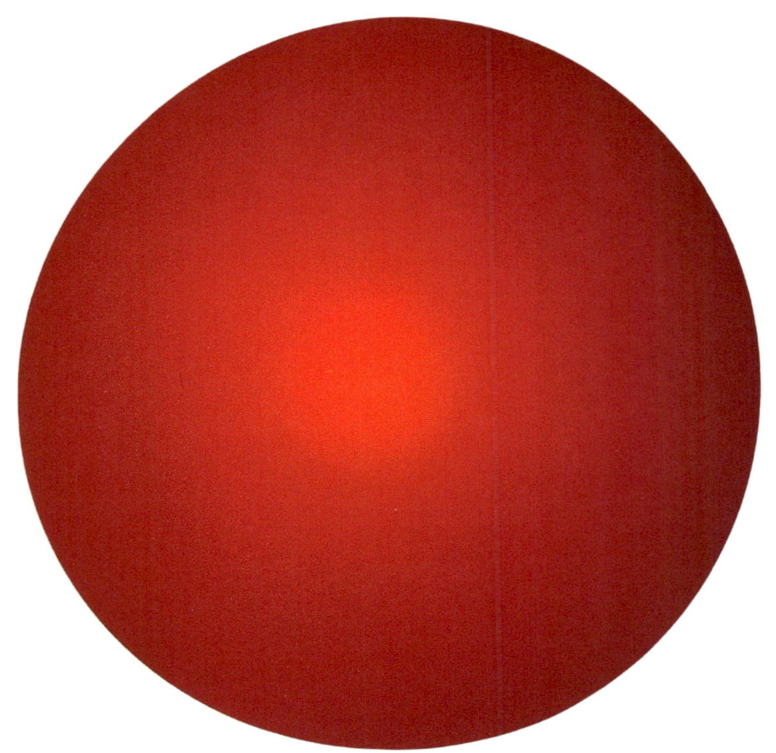

Tondo 28, 1970, acrylic on canvas, 48" diameter

Tondo 32, 1970, acrylic on canvas, 48" diameter

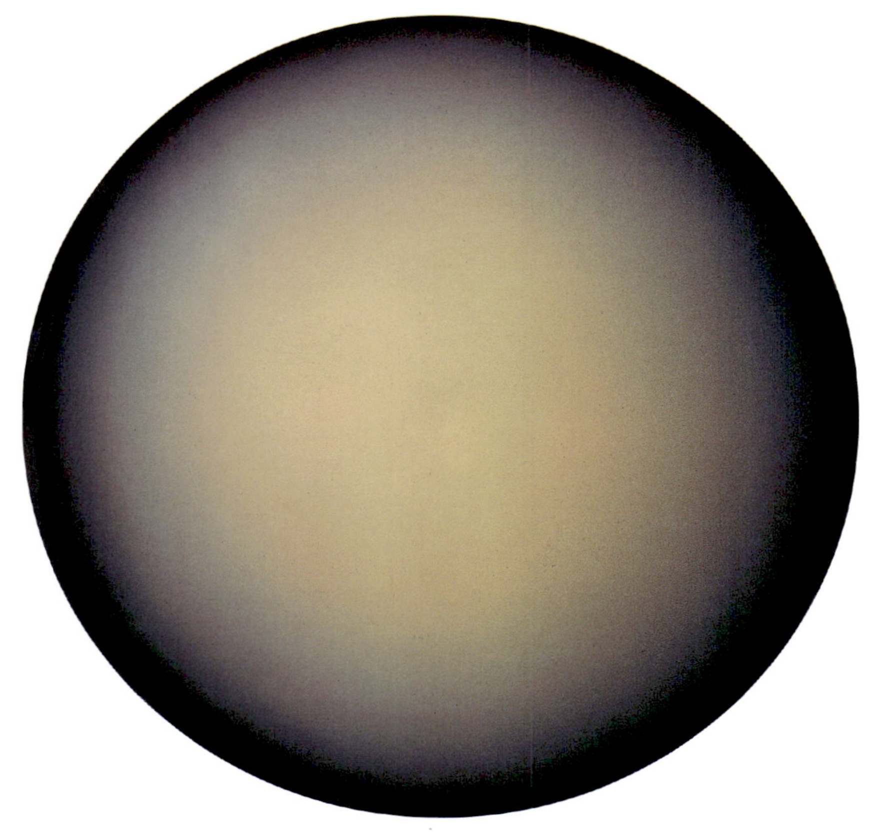

TONDO SERIES

Tondo 26, 1970, acrylic on canvas, 48" diameter

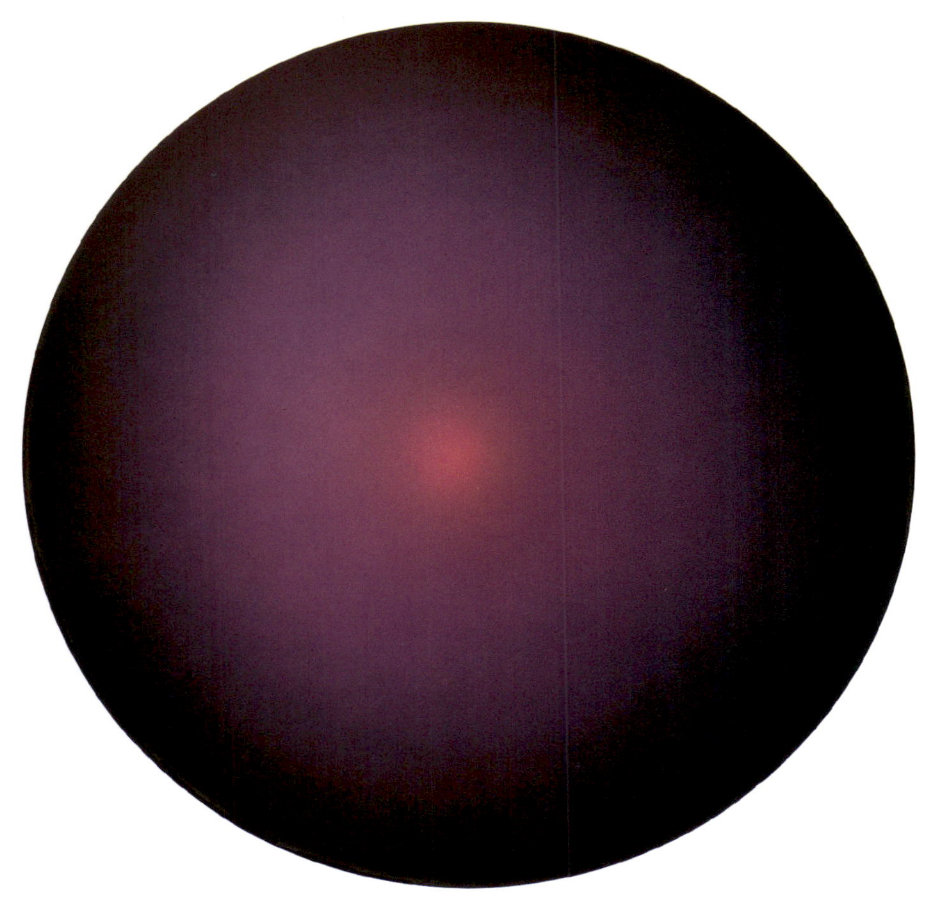

TONDO SERIES

Tondo 34, 1971, acrylic on canvas, 72" diameter

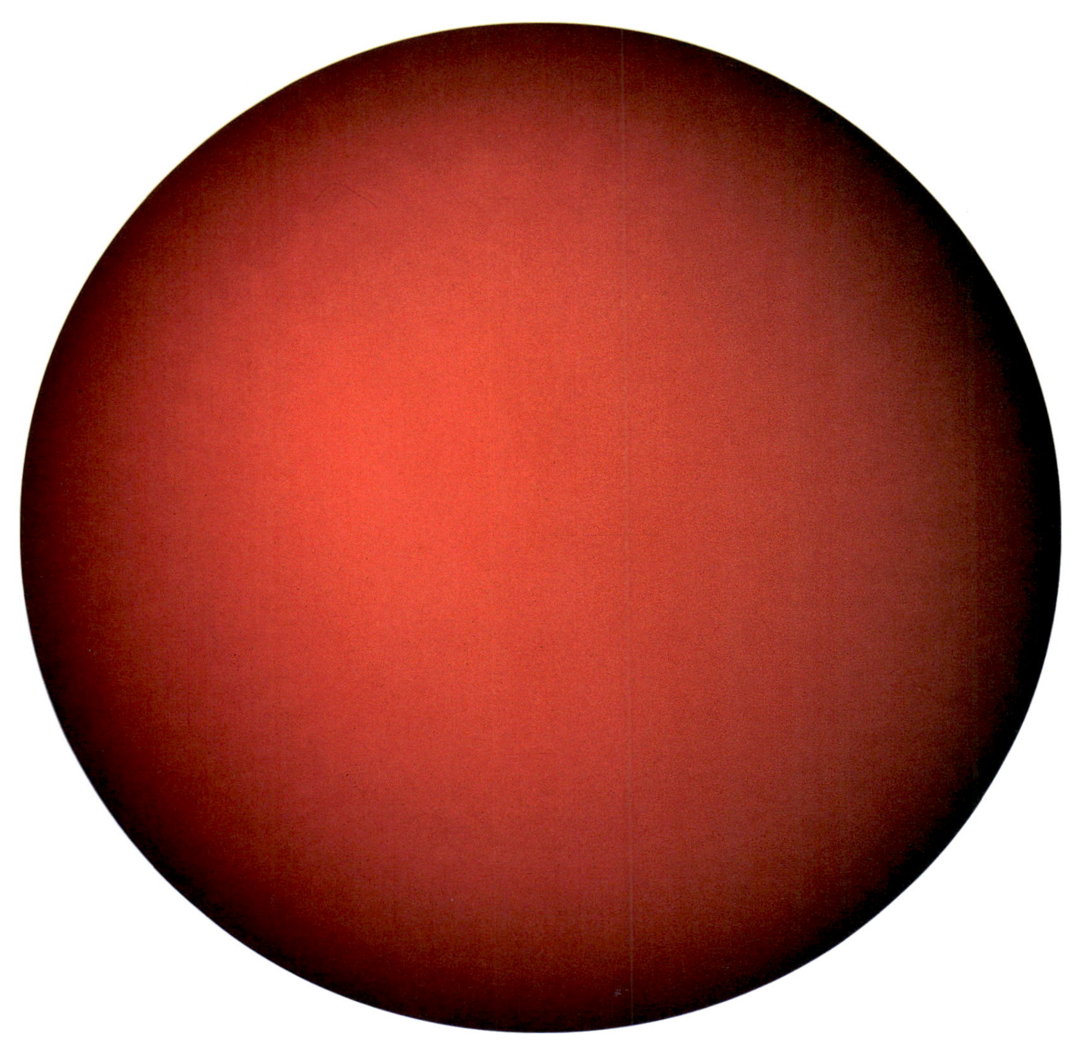

TONDO SERIES

Tondo 38, 1971, acrylic on canvas, 72" diameter

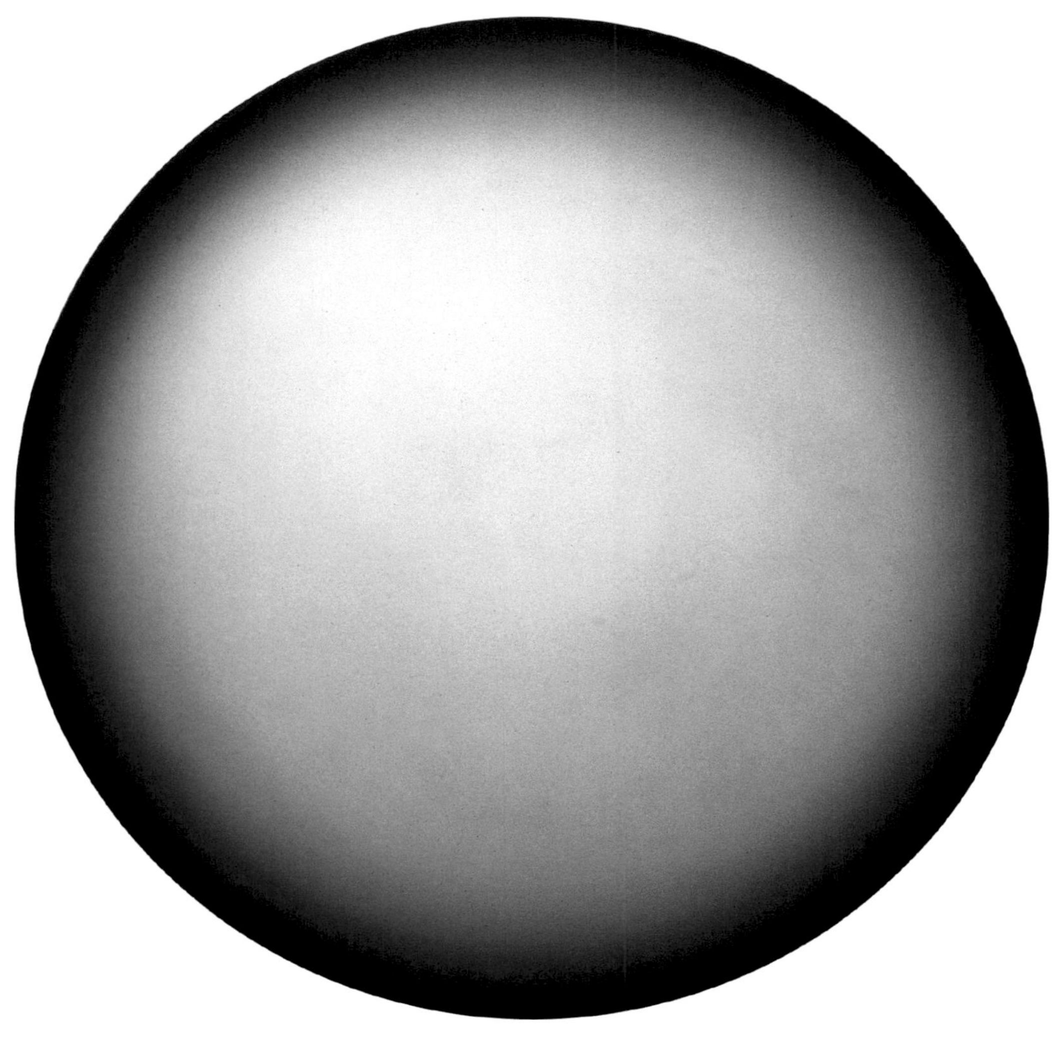

TONDO SERIES

Tondo 39, 1971, acrylic on canvas, 72" diameter

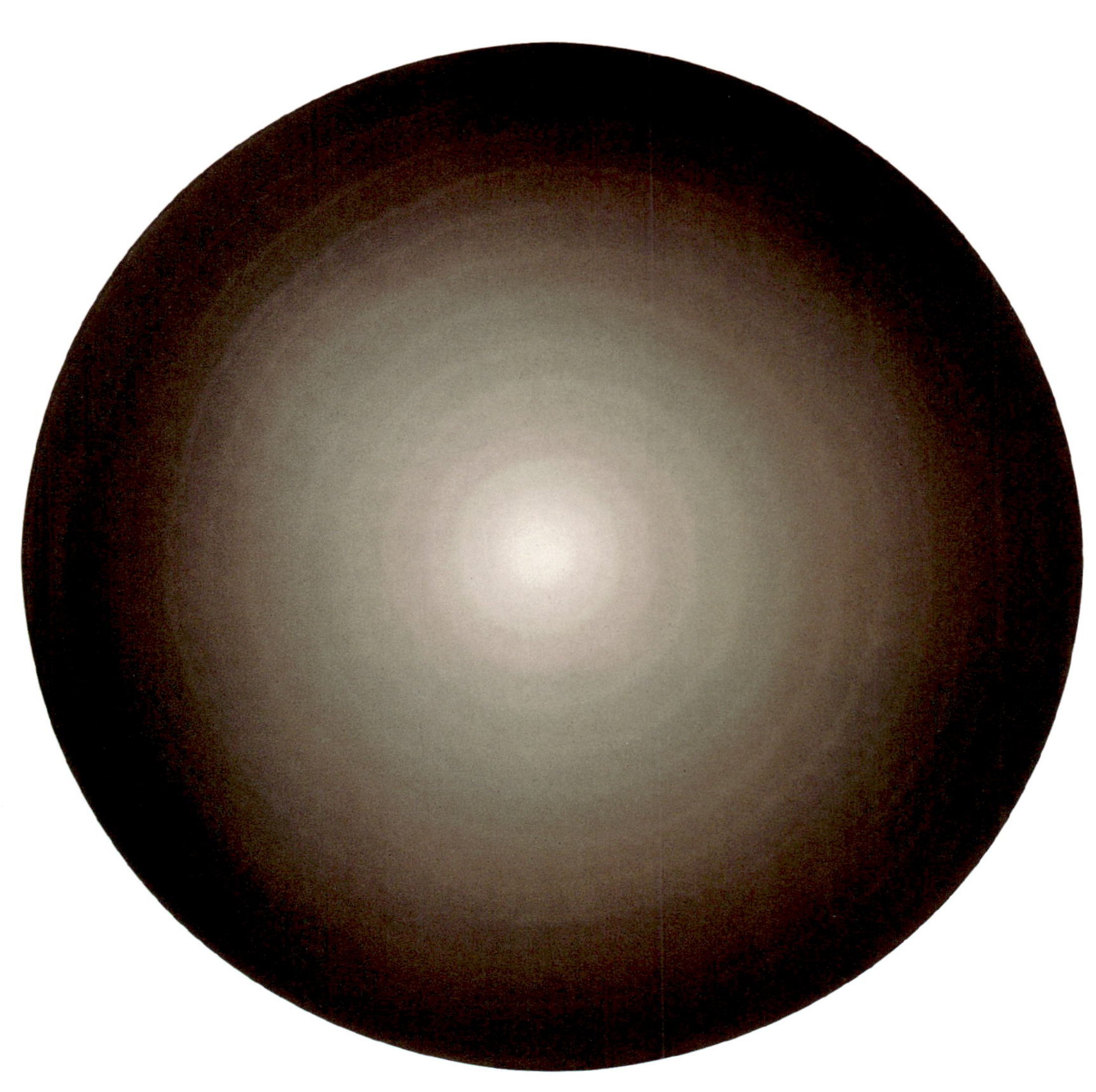

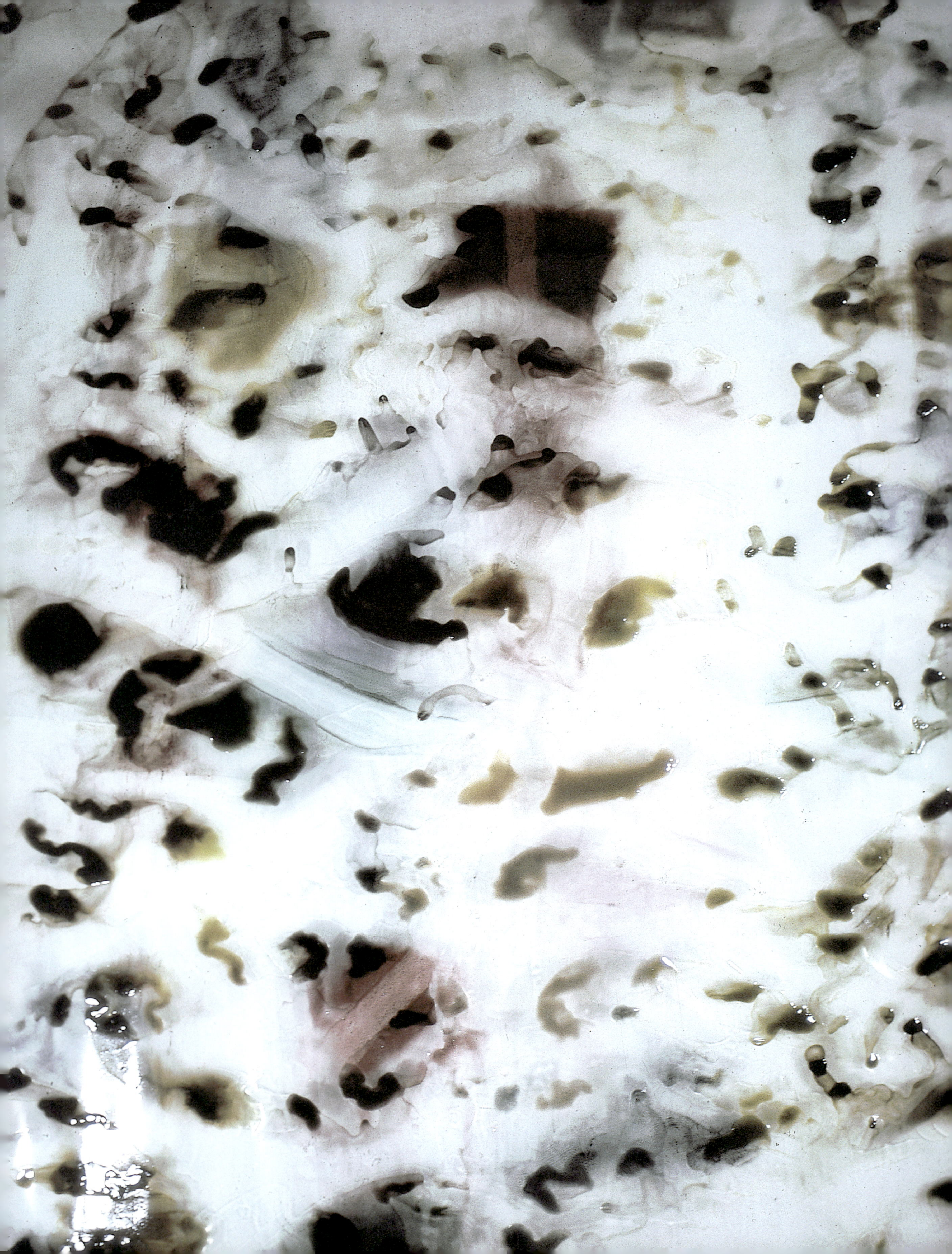

VERTICAL SCROLL SERIES

Untitled 12, 1971, polyurethene and powdered pigment, 144" x 48"

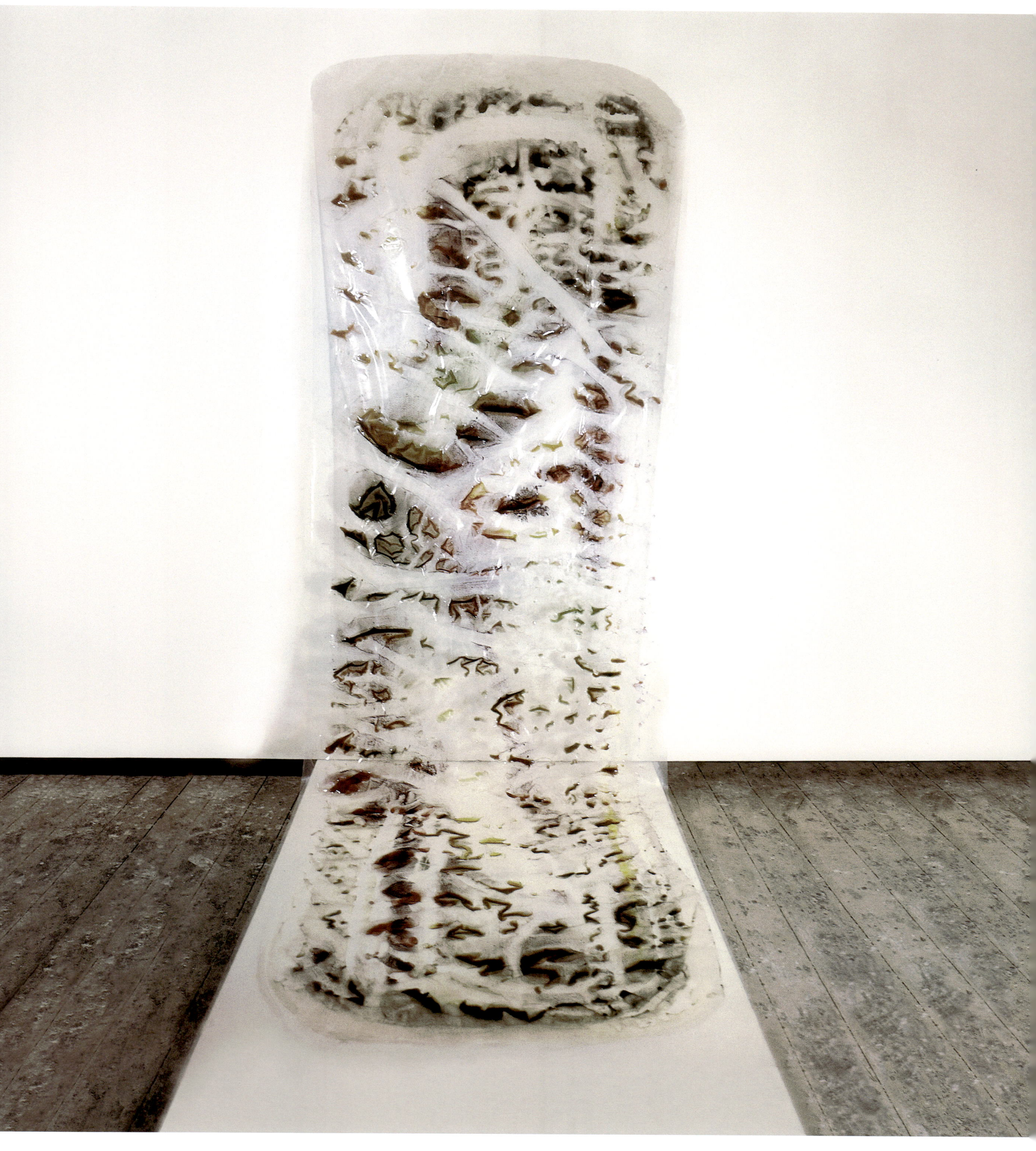

VERTICAL SCROLL SERIES

Untitled 4, 1971, polyurethene and powdered pigment, 96" x 24"

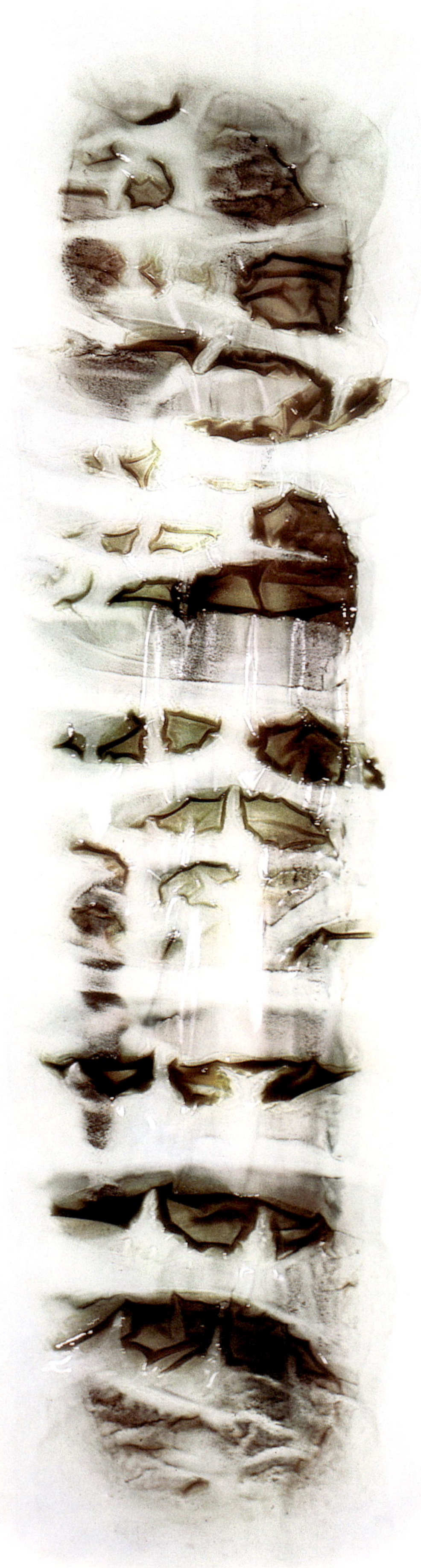

Vertical Scroll 16, 1972, acrylic, gauze, rhoplex, 84" x 36"

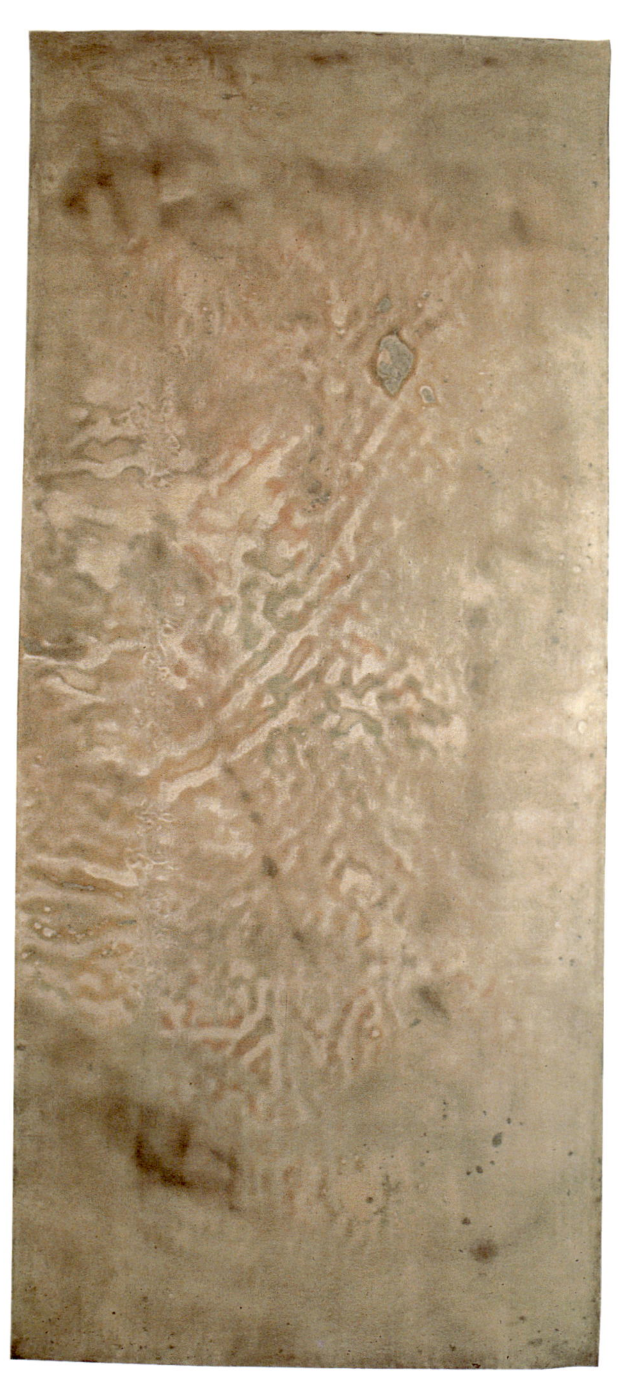

VERTICAL SCROLL SERIES

Vertical Scroll 20, 1972, acrylic, gauze, rhoplex, 84" x 36"

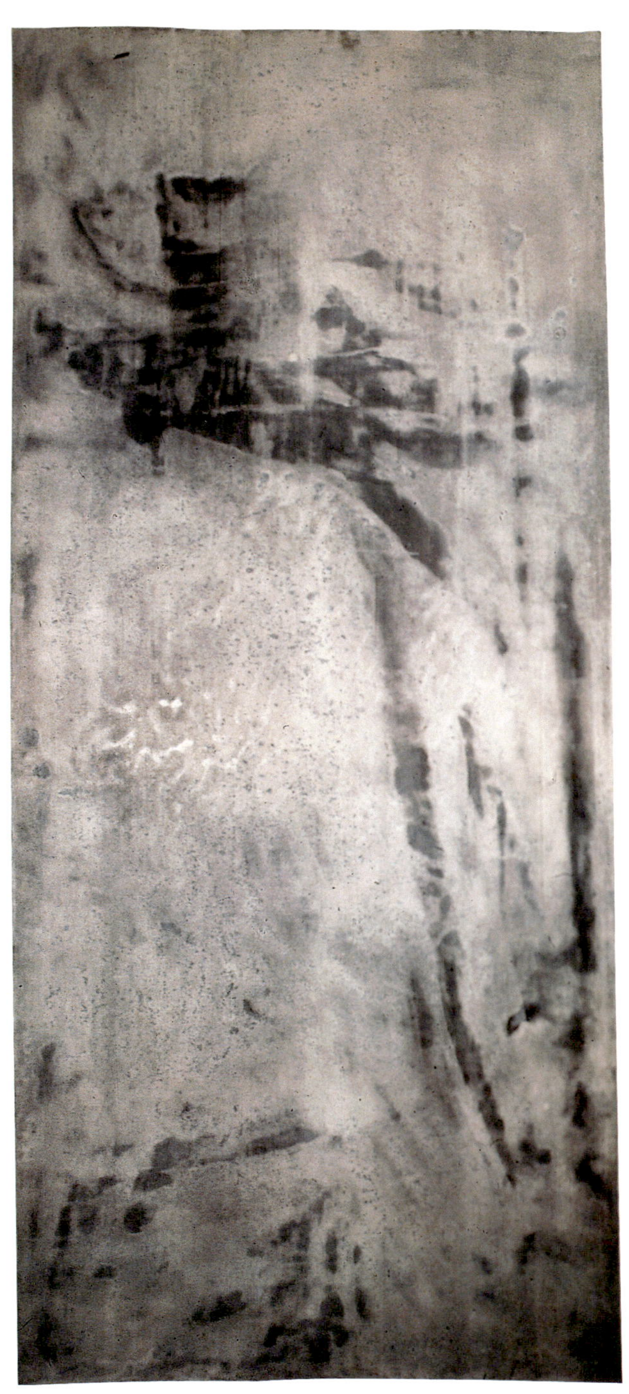

Vertical Scroll 19, 1972, acrylic, gauze, rhoplex, 84" x 36"

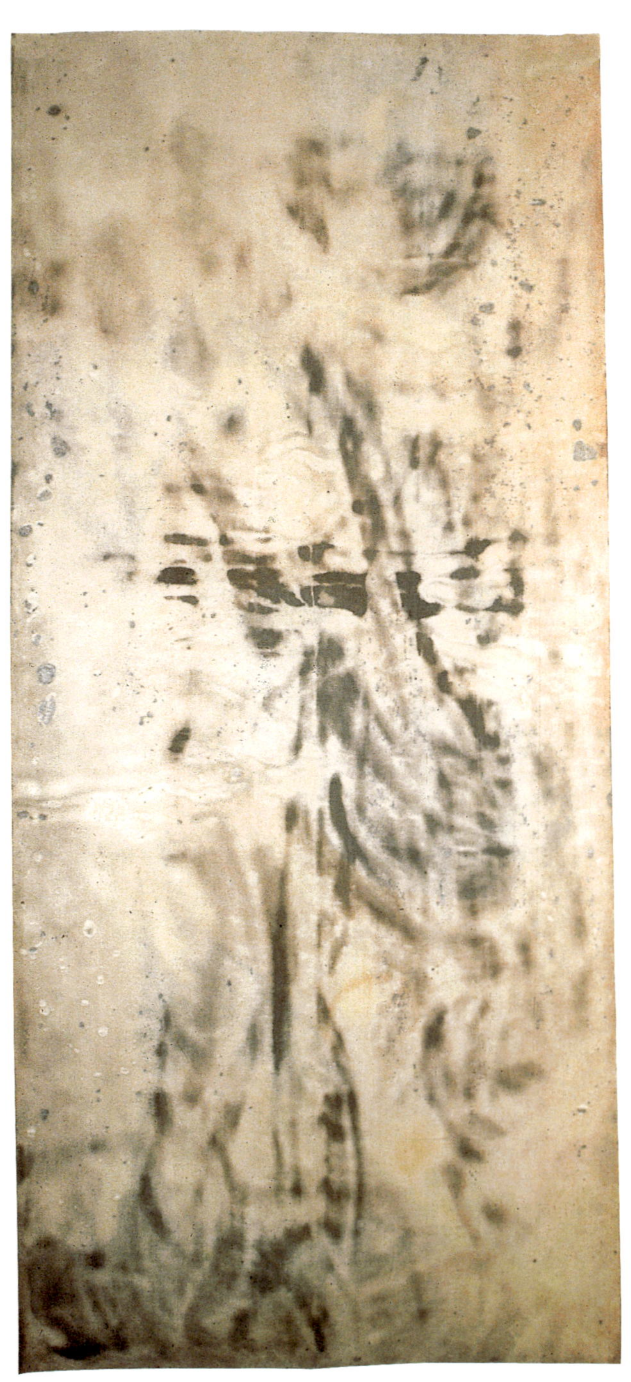

VERTICAL SCROLL SERIES

Vertical Scroll 24, 1973, acrylic, gauze, rhoplex, 84" x 36"

CIRCLE SERIES

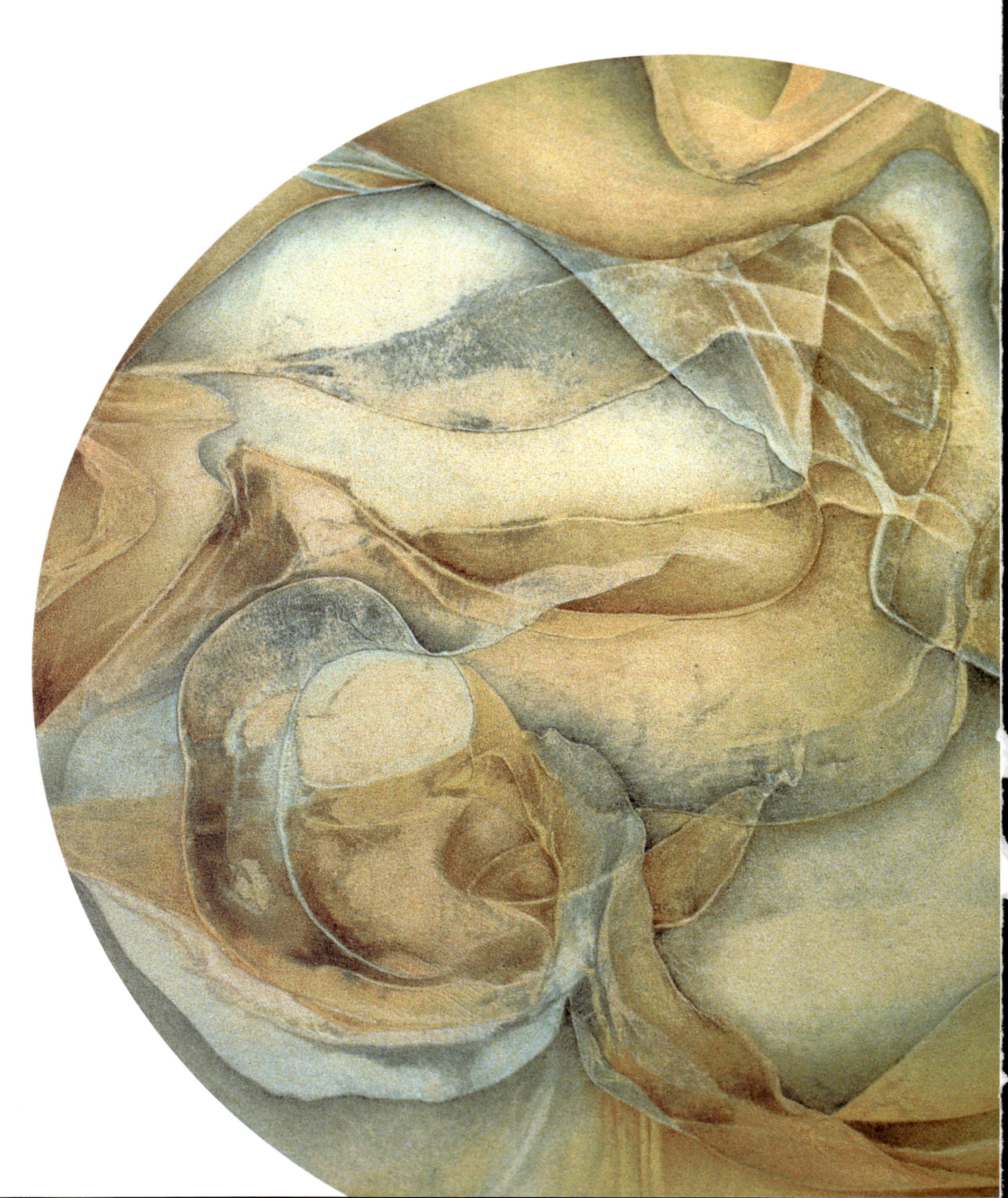

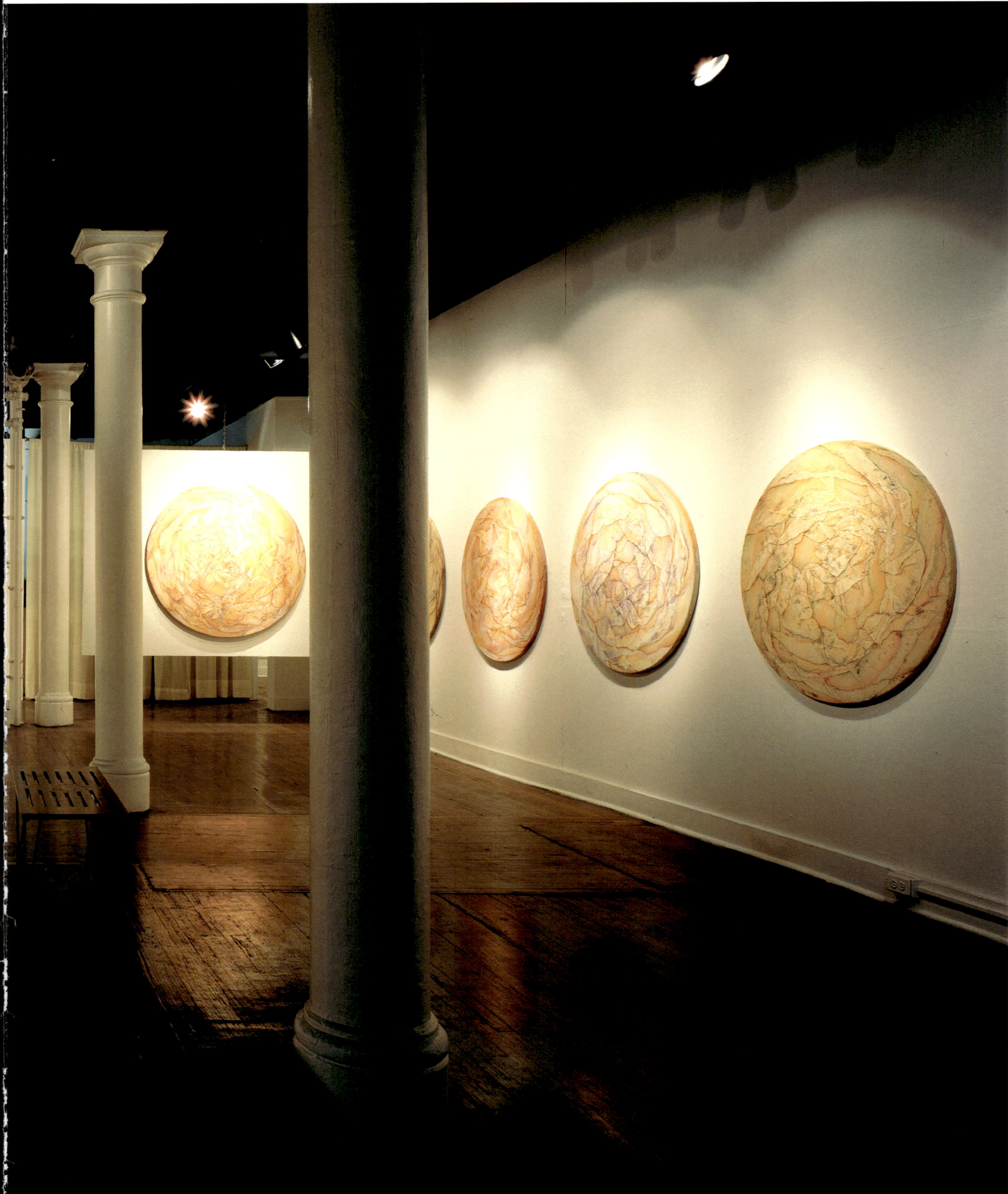

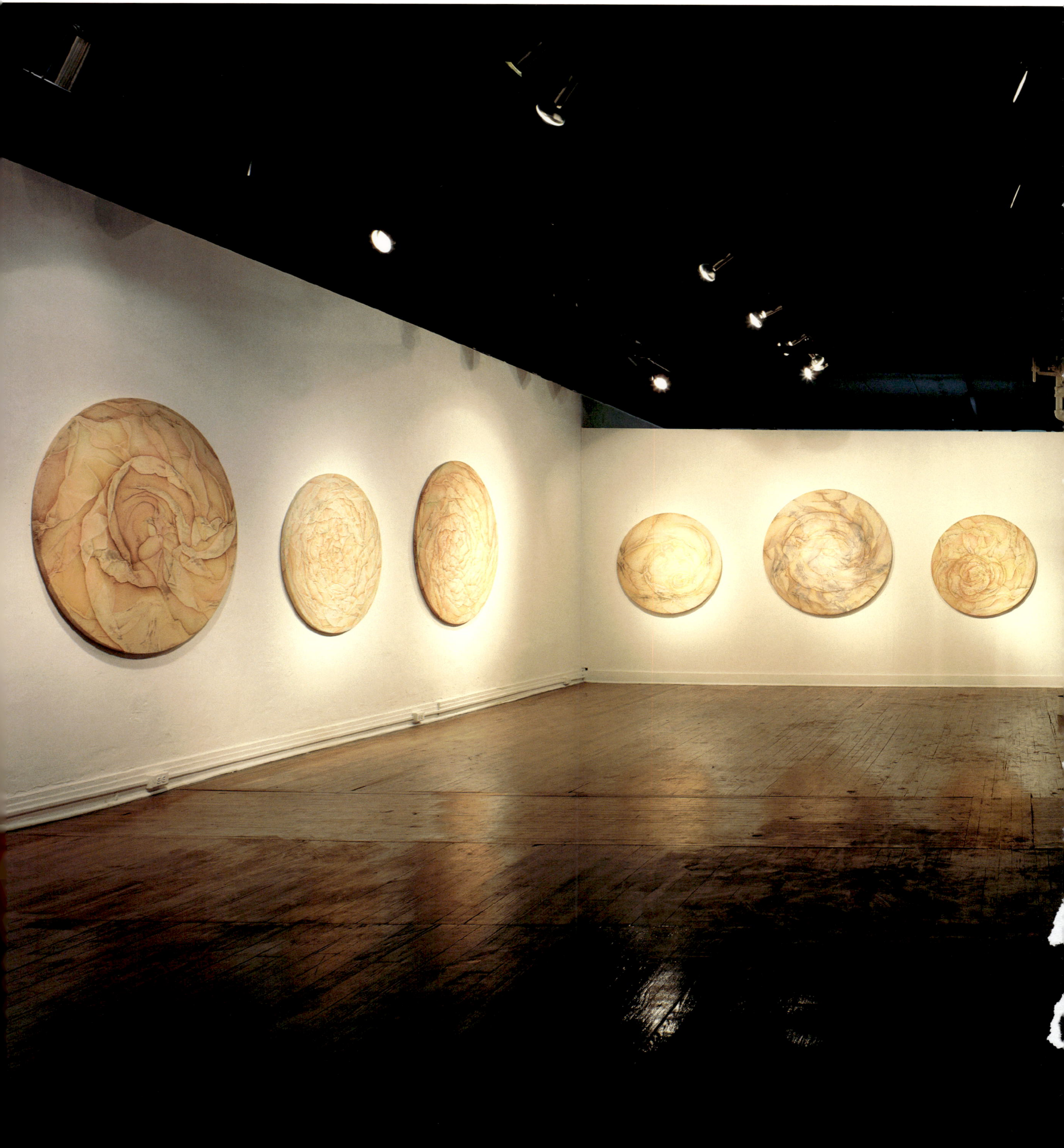

Installation View, Soho 20, New York, New York, 1979

CIRCLE SERIES

Circle 41, 1978, acrylic, gauze, rhoplex, 60" diameter

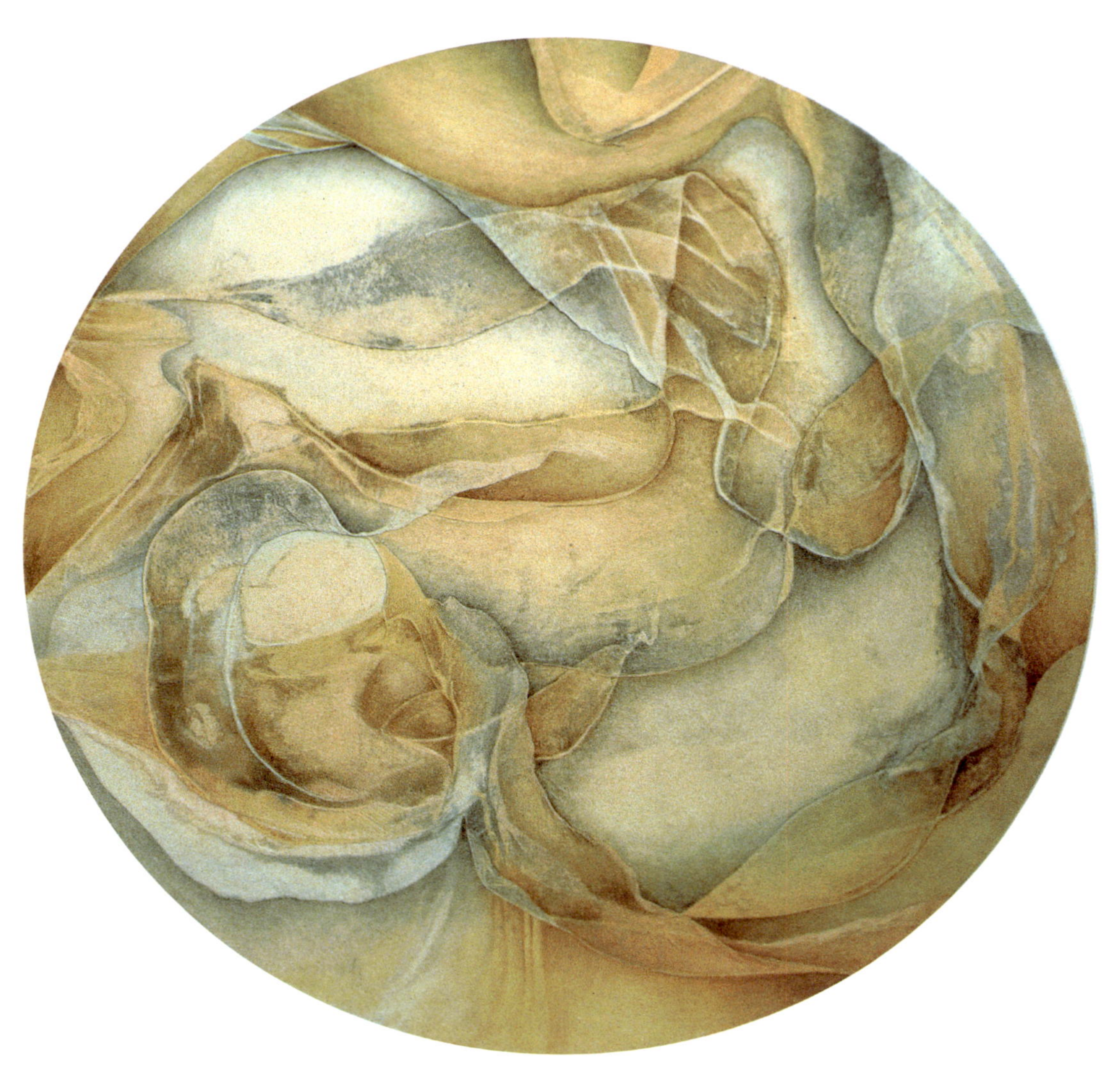

CIRCLE SERIES

Appassionata, 1979, acrylic, gauze, rhoplex, 59" diameter

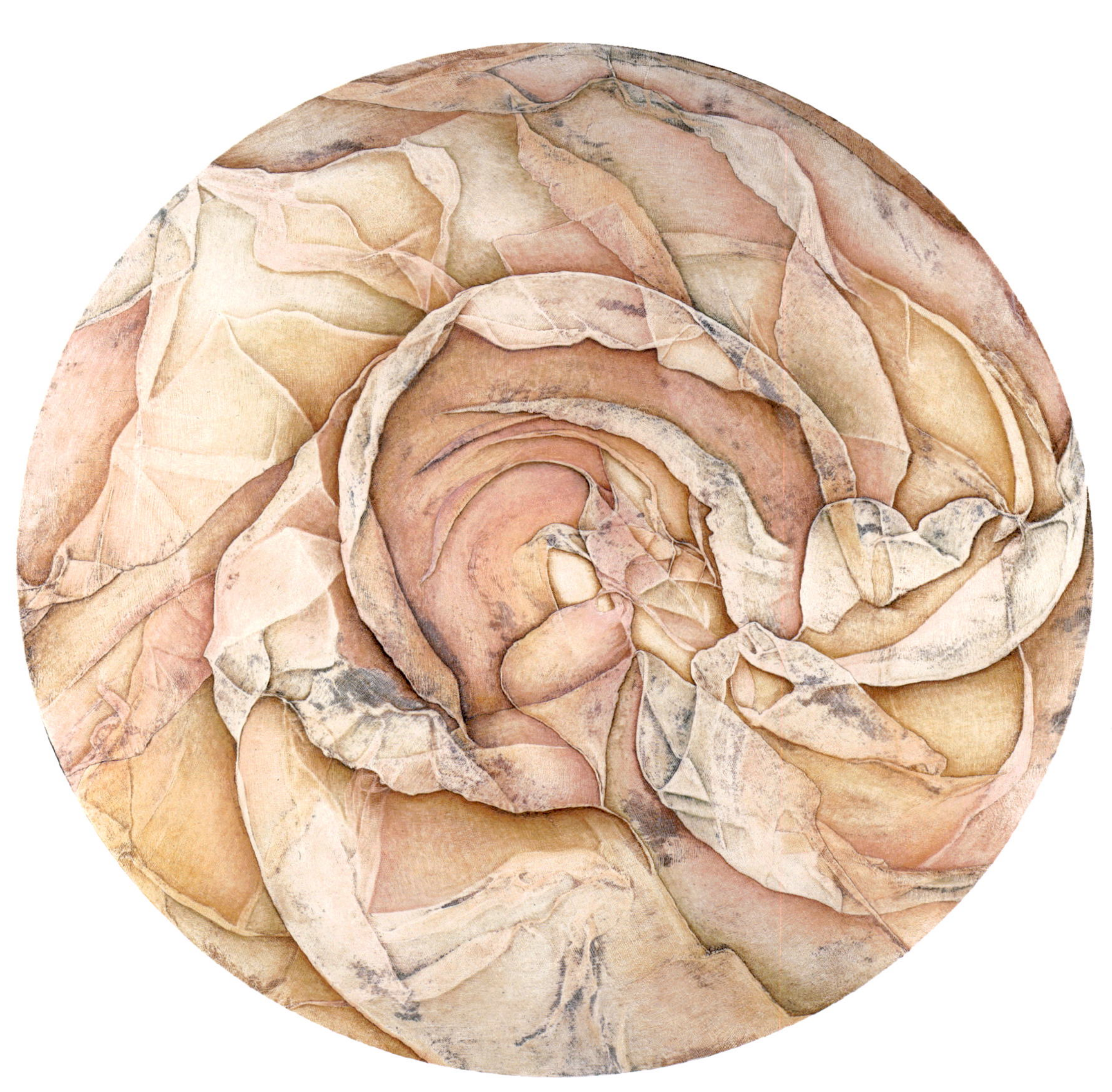

CIRCLE SERIES

Calyx II, 1980, acrylic, gauze, rhoplex, 48" diameter

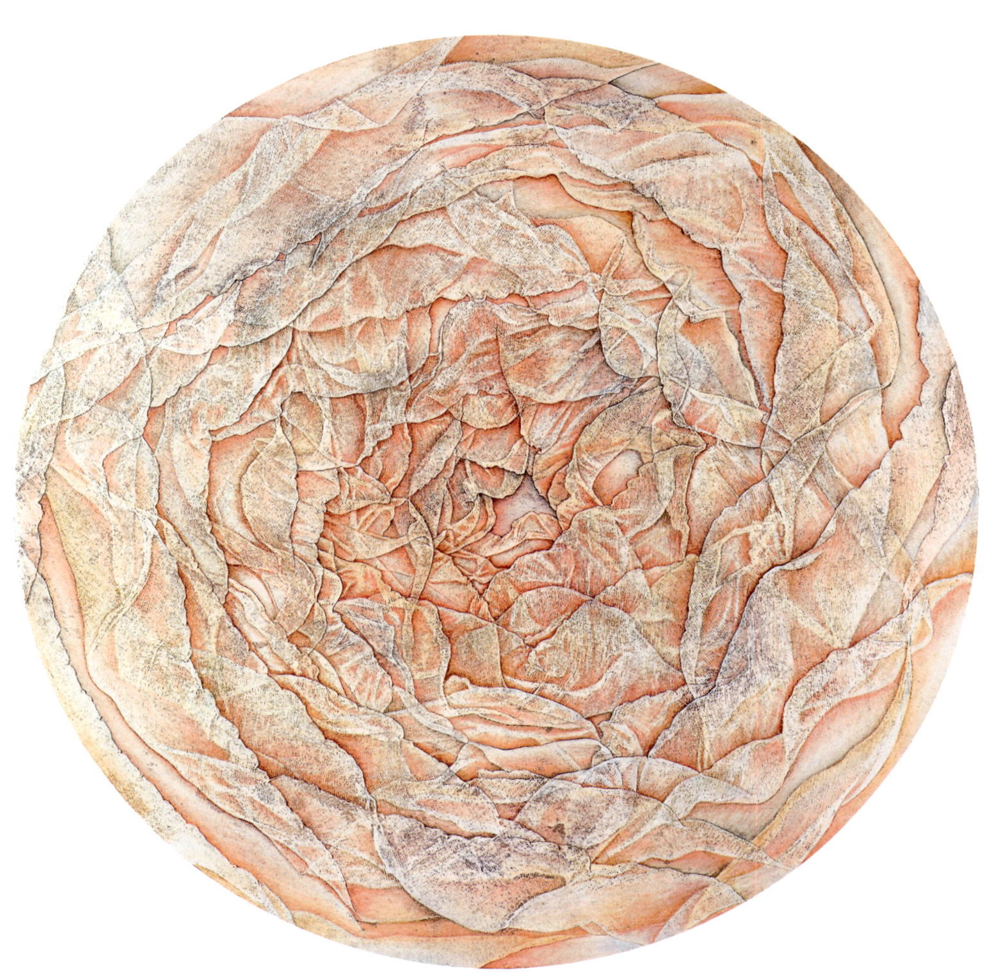

CIRCLE SERIES

Return Inward, 1982, acrylic, gauze, rhoplex, 48" diameter

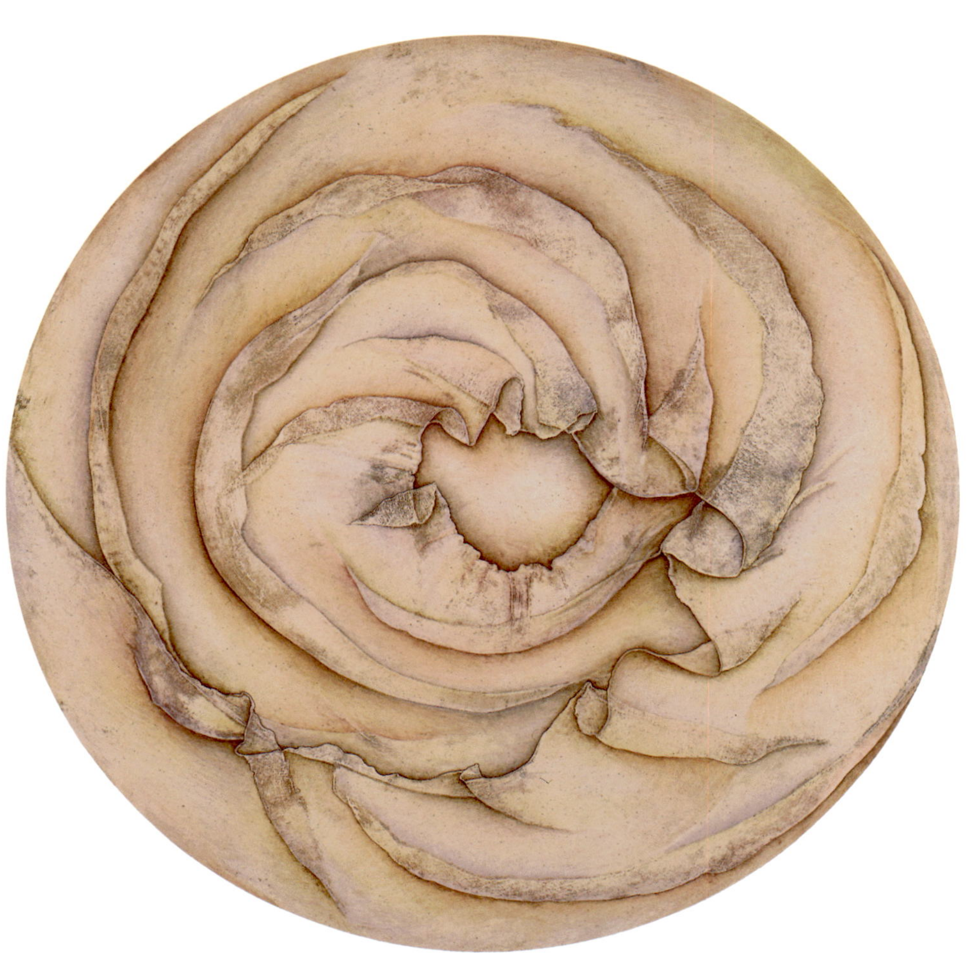

CIRCLE SERIES

Dark Entry, 1982, acrylic, gauze, rhoplex, 59" diameter

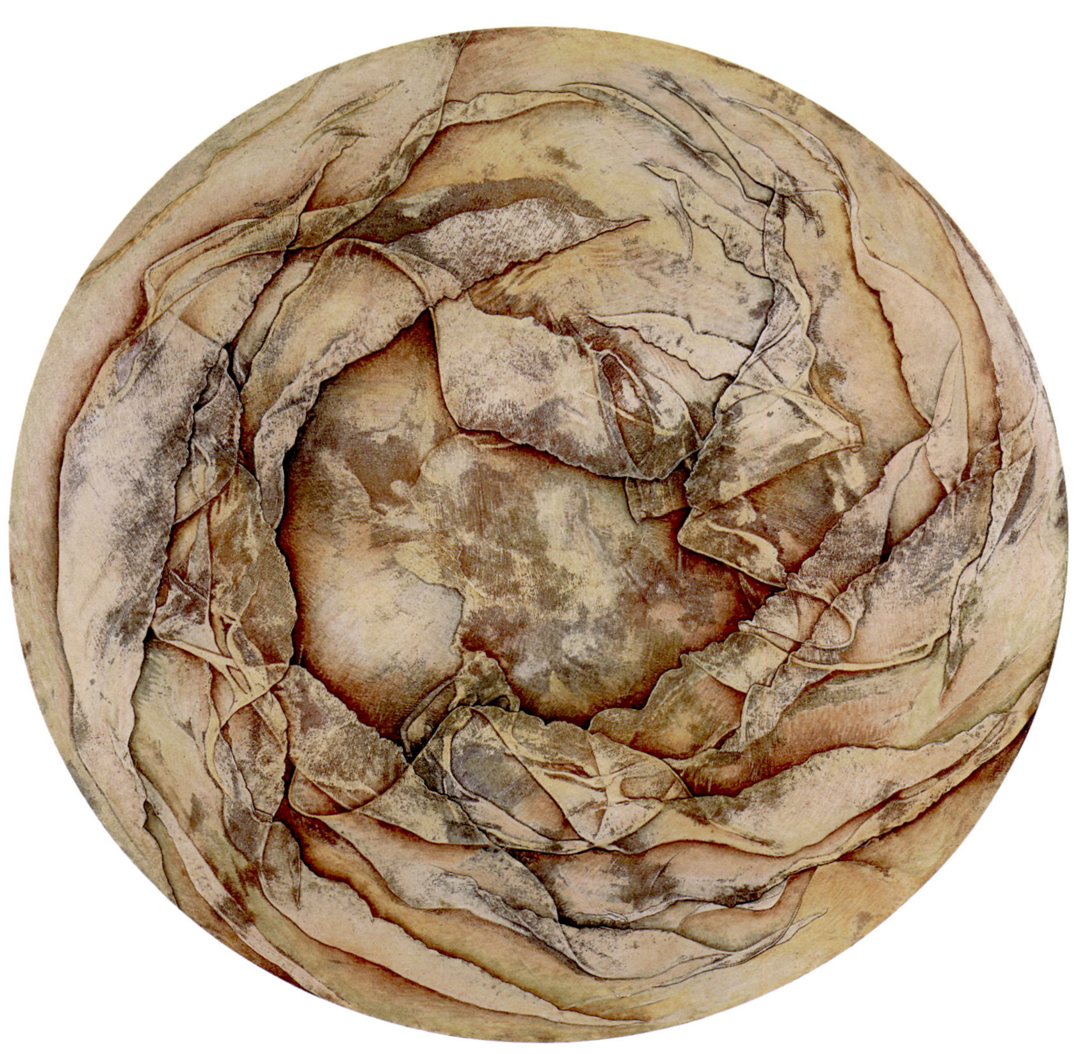

CIRCLE SERIES

Luminare, 1982, acrylic, gauze, rhoplex, 59" diameter

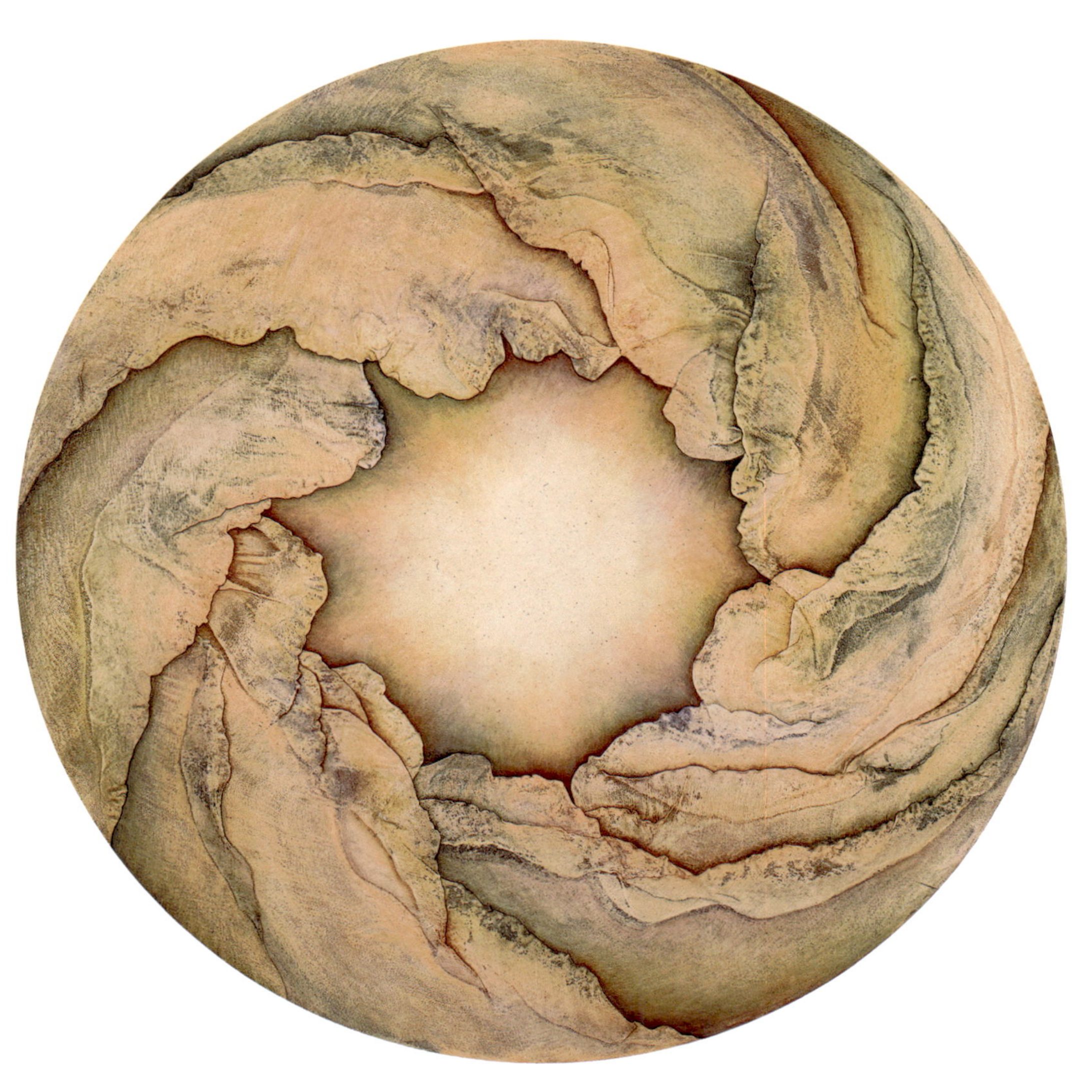

CIRCLE SERIES

Void Unveiled, 1983, acrylic, gauze, rhoplex, 60" diameter

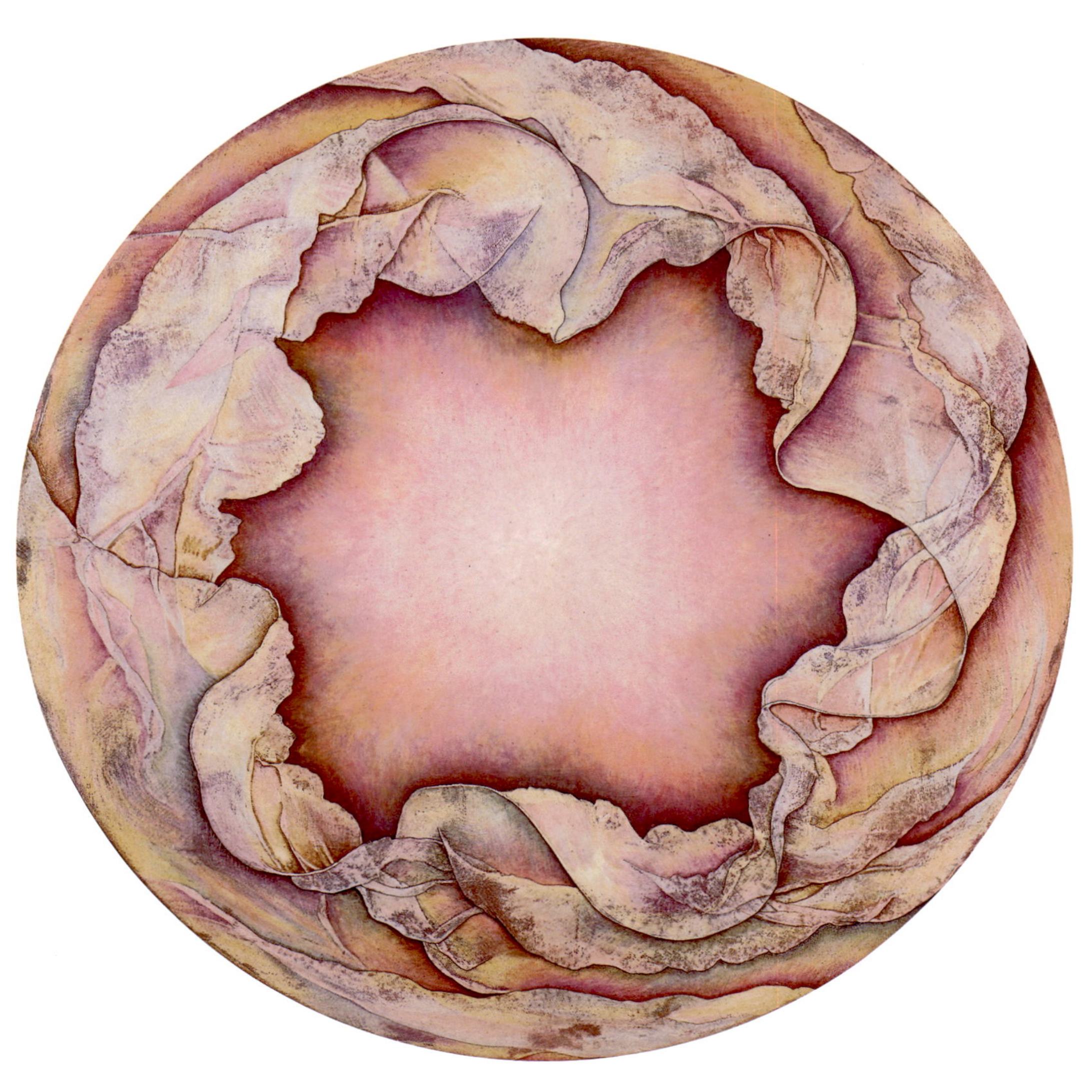

CIRCLE SERIES

Circle of Light, 1983, acrylic, gauze, rhoplex, 72" diameter

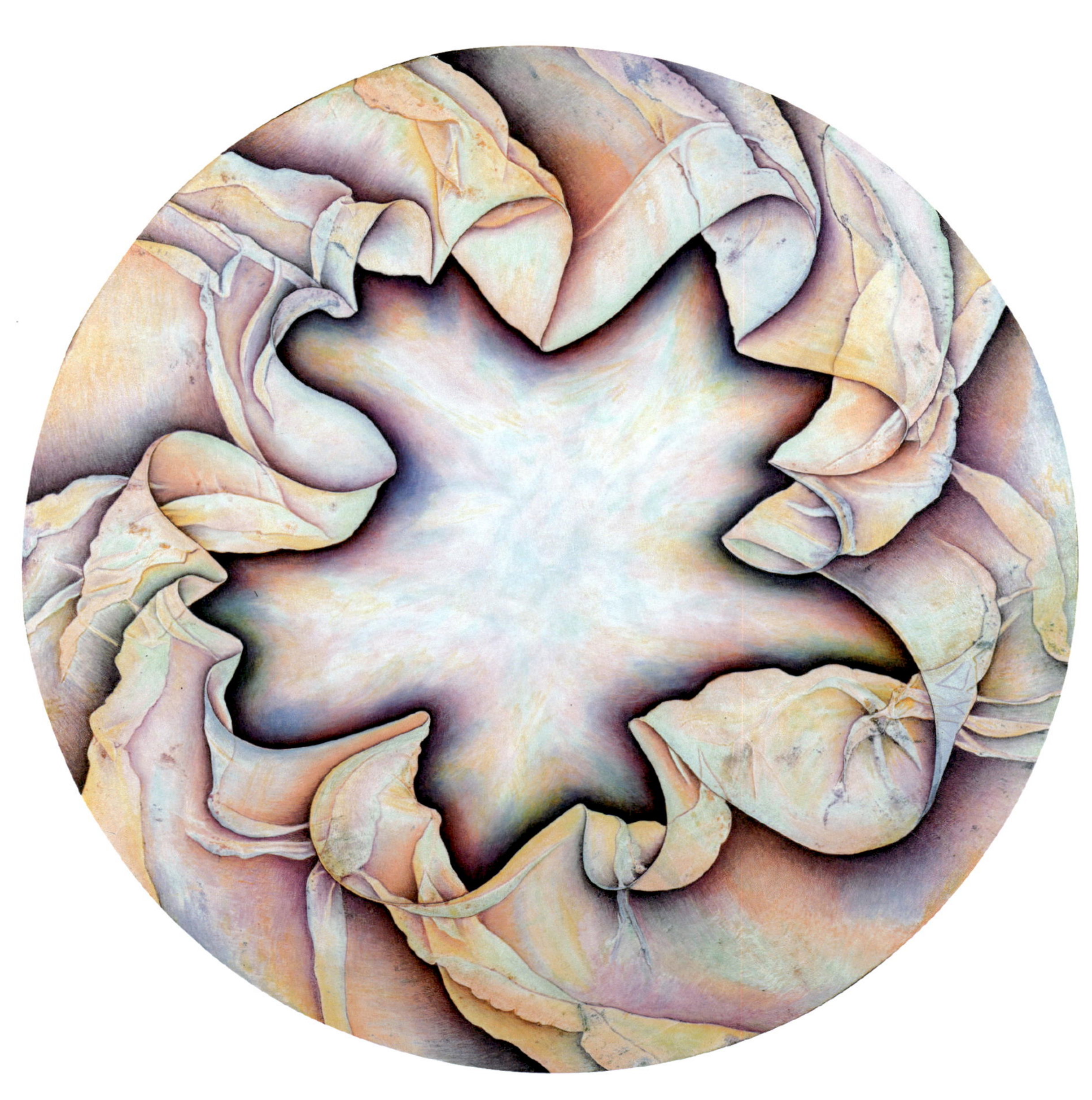

WALL HANGING SERIES

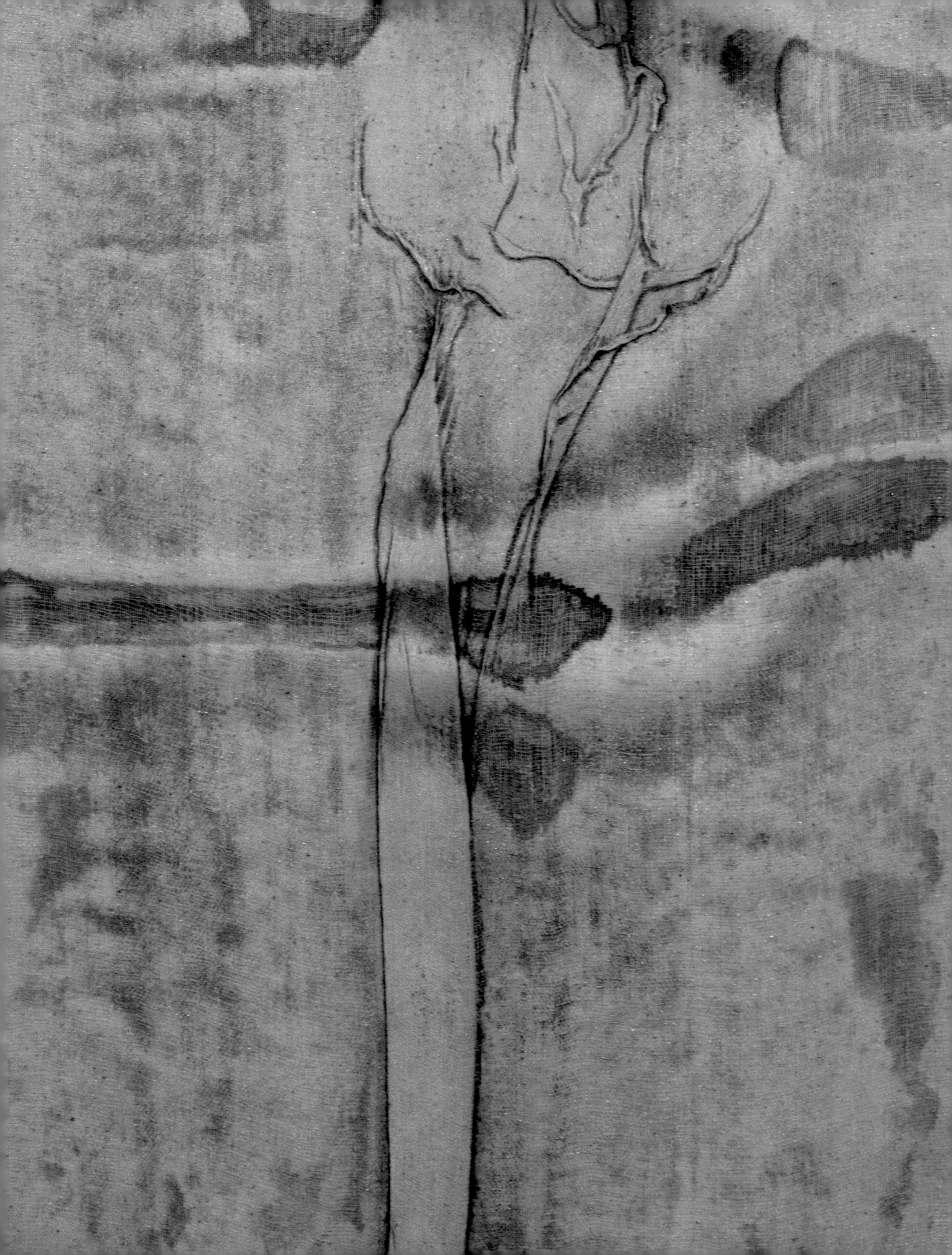

WALL HANGING SERIES

Wall Hanging 1, 1978, acrylic, gauze, rhoplex, 82" x 18"

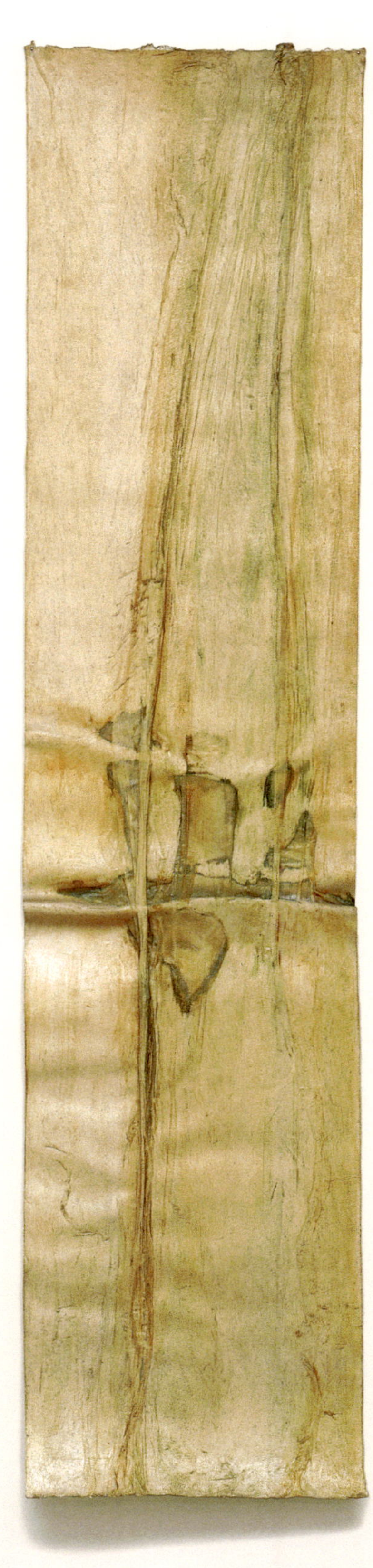

WALL HANGING SERIES

Wall Hanging 5, 1981, acrylic, gauze, rhoplex, 72" x 24"

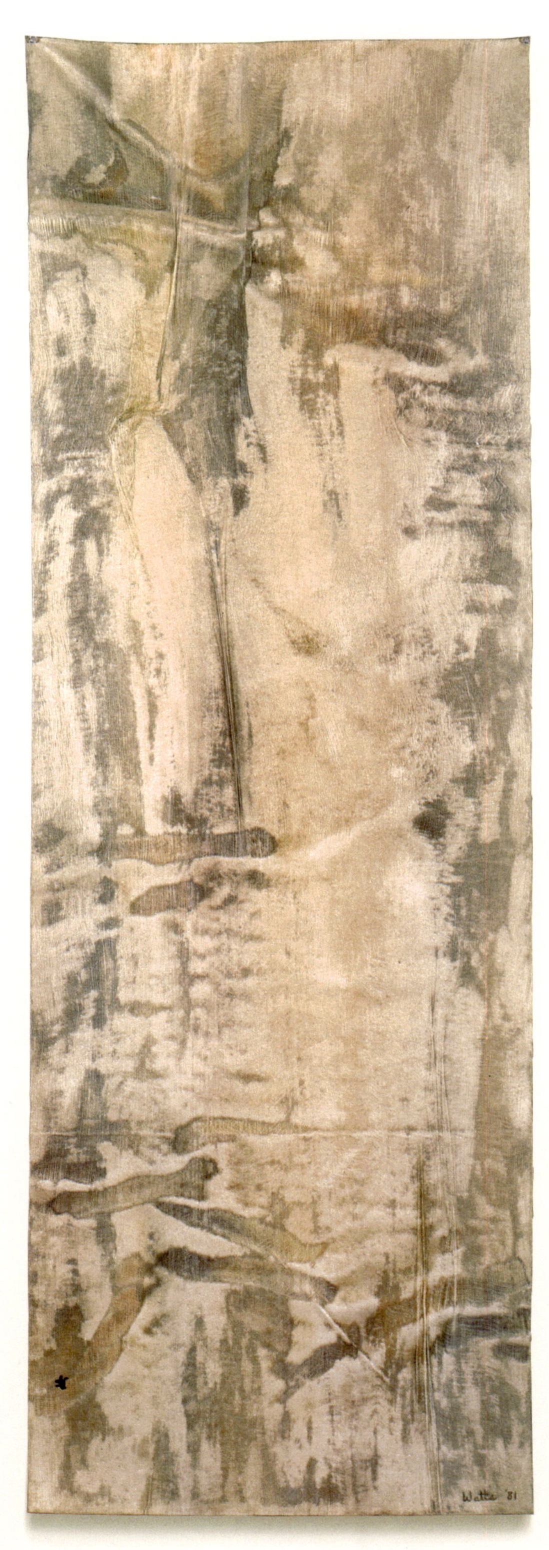

Wall Hanging 20, 1981, acrylic, gauze, rhoplex, 72" x 24"

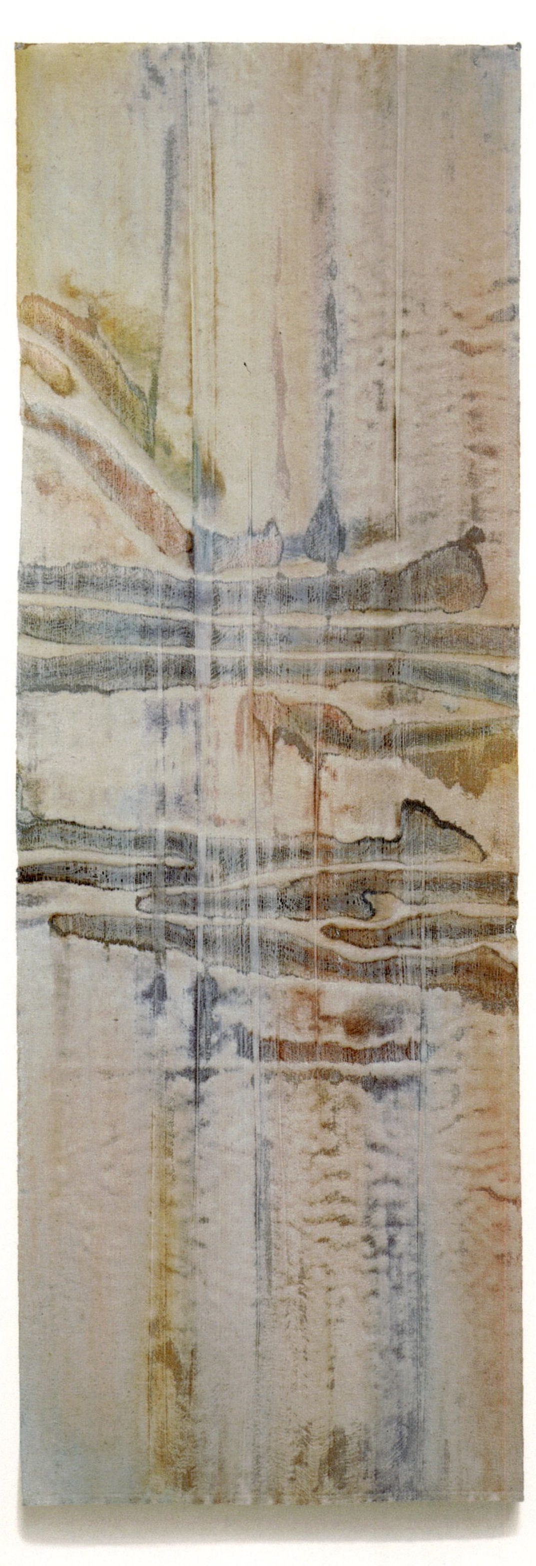

WALL HANGING SERIES

Wall Hanging 39, 1982, acrylic, gauze, rhoplex, 72" x 24"

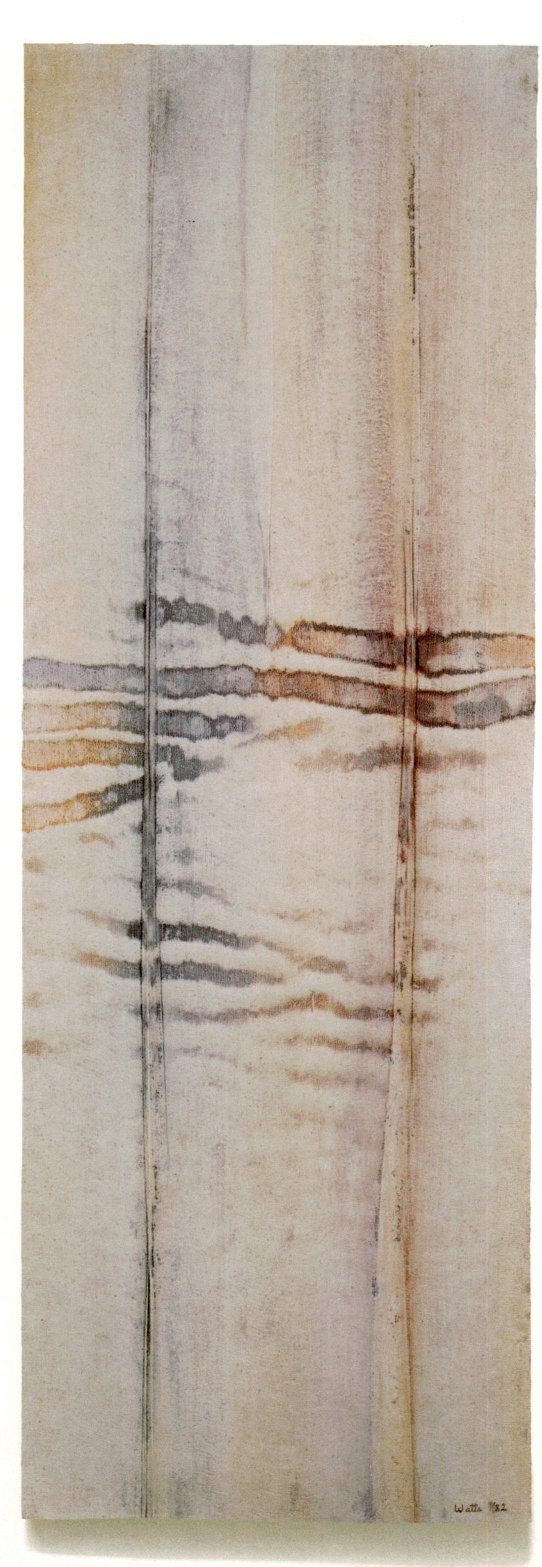

WALL HANGING SERIES

Wall Hanging 40, 1982, acrylic, gauze, rhoplex, 72" x 24"

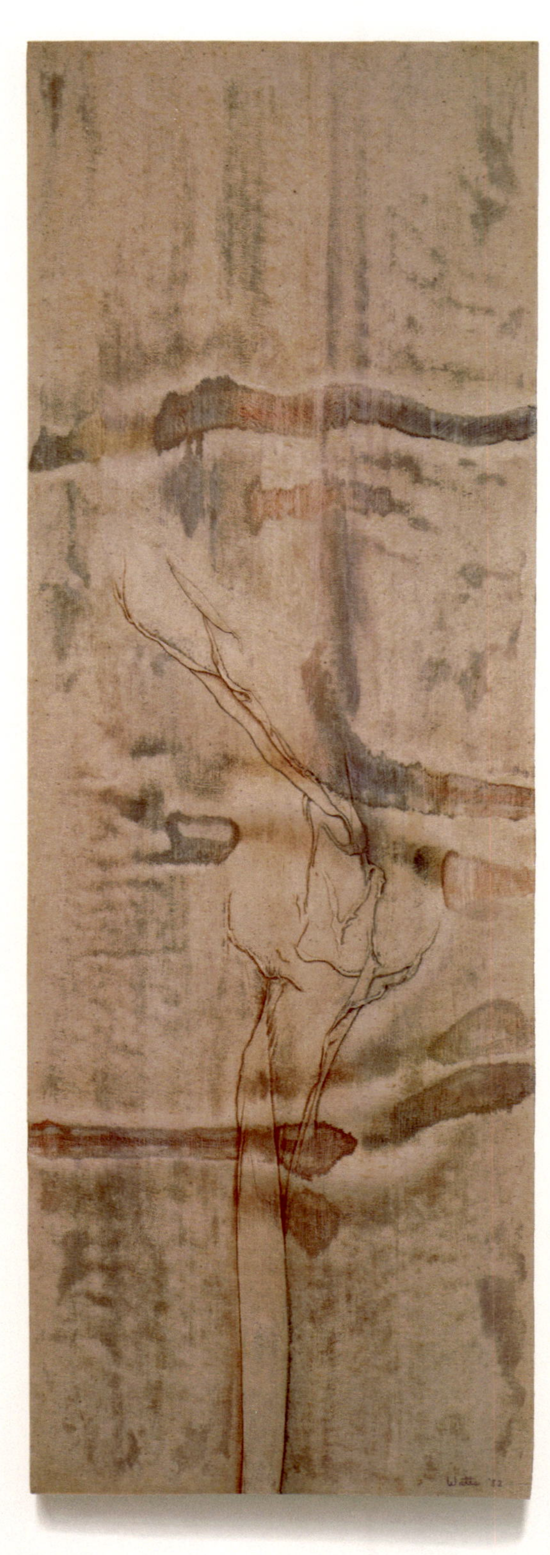

WALL HANGING SERIES

Taos, 1984, acrylic, gauze, rhoplex, 72" x 24"

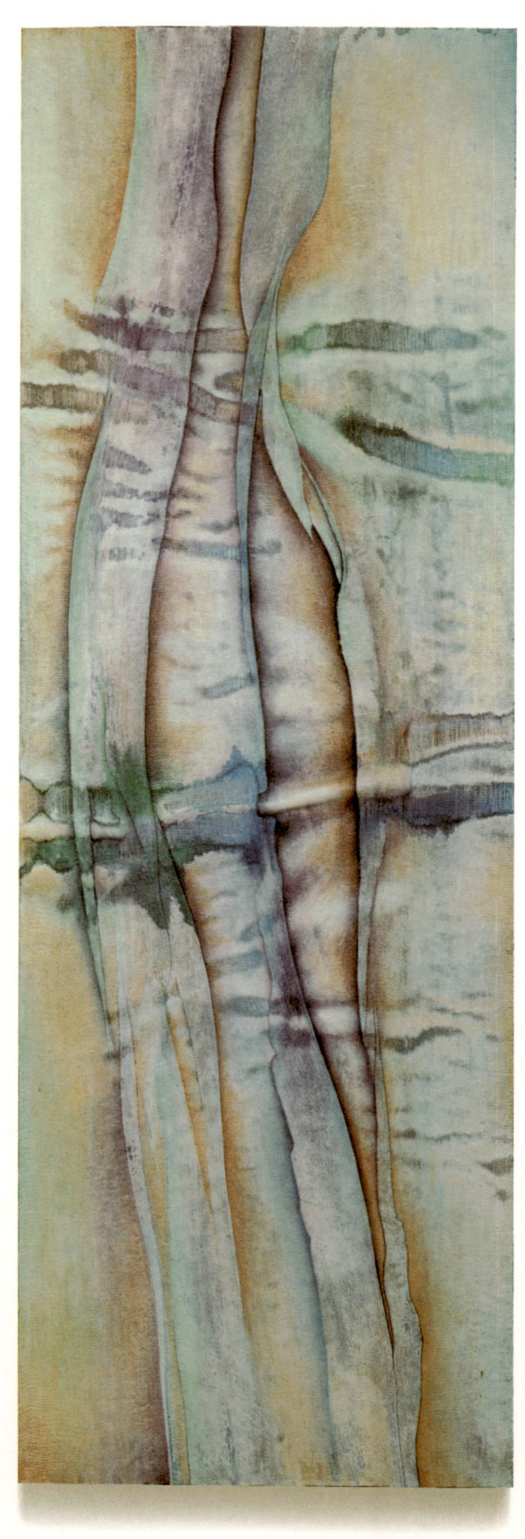

LANDSCAPE 1 SERIES

Early Morning Light, 1987, oil and pastel on paper, 12.25" x 16"

LANDSCAPE 1 SERIES

Inner Canyon, 1987, oil and pastel on paper, 12.25" x 16"

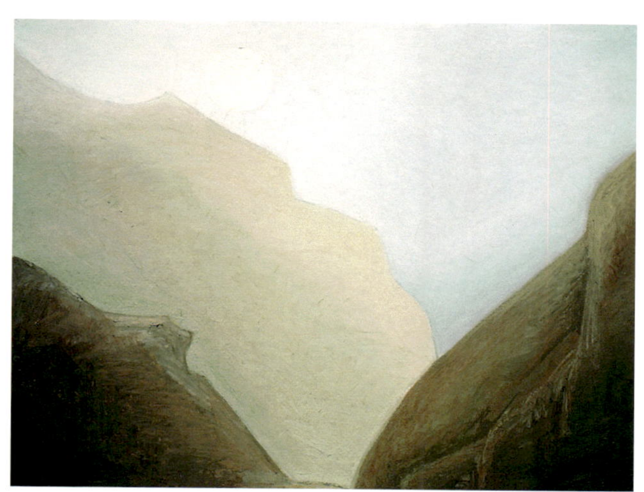

LANDSCAPE 1 SERIES

White Light, 1987, acrylic on canvas, 48" x 84"

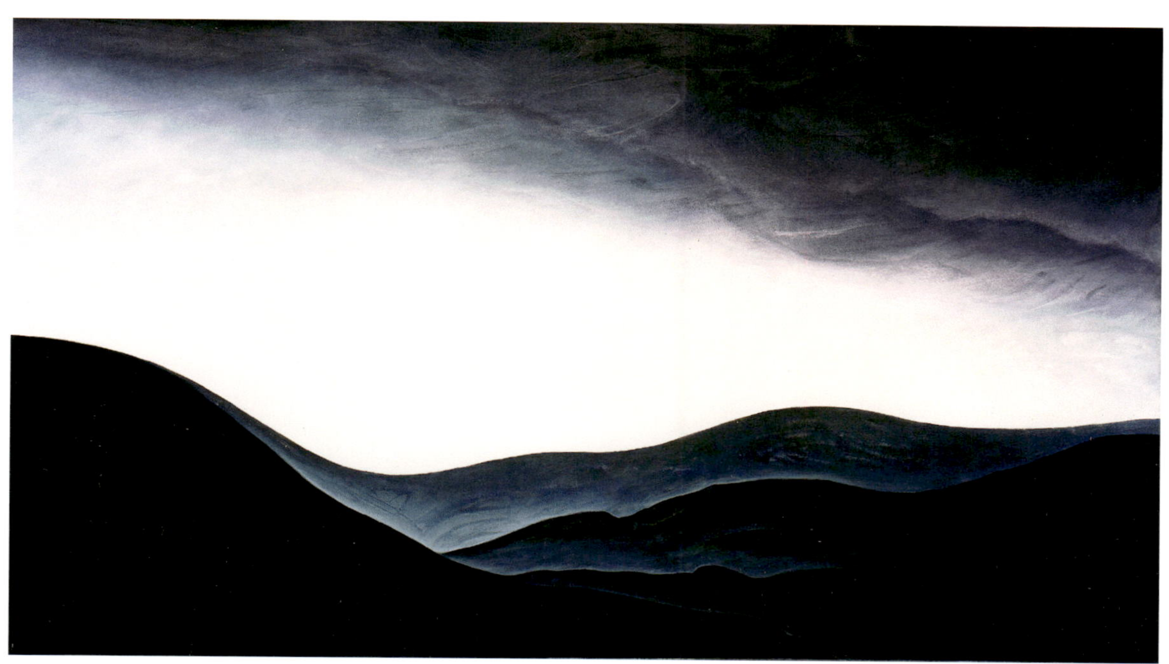

LANDSCAPE 1 SERIES

White Light over Jemez, 1988, oil and pastel on paper, 12.25" x 16"

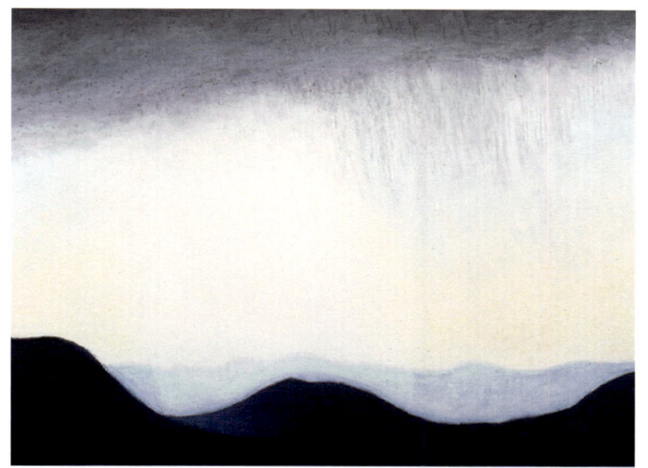

LANDSCAPE 1 SERIES

First Light II, 1988, oil and pastel on paper, 12.25" x 16"

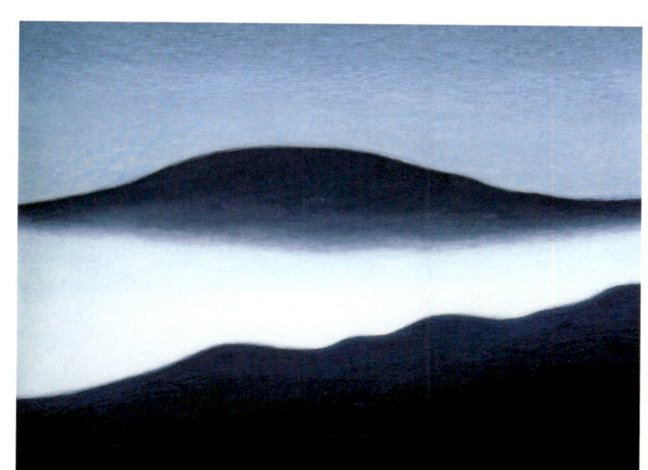

LANDSCAPE 1 SERIES

Blue Notch, 1989, oil on canvas, 60" x 42"

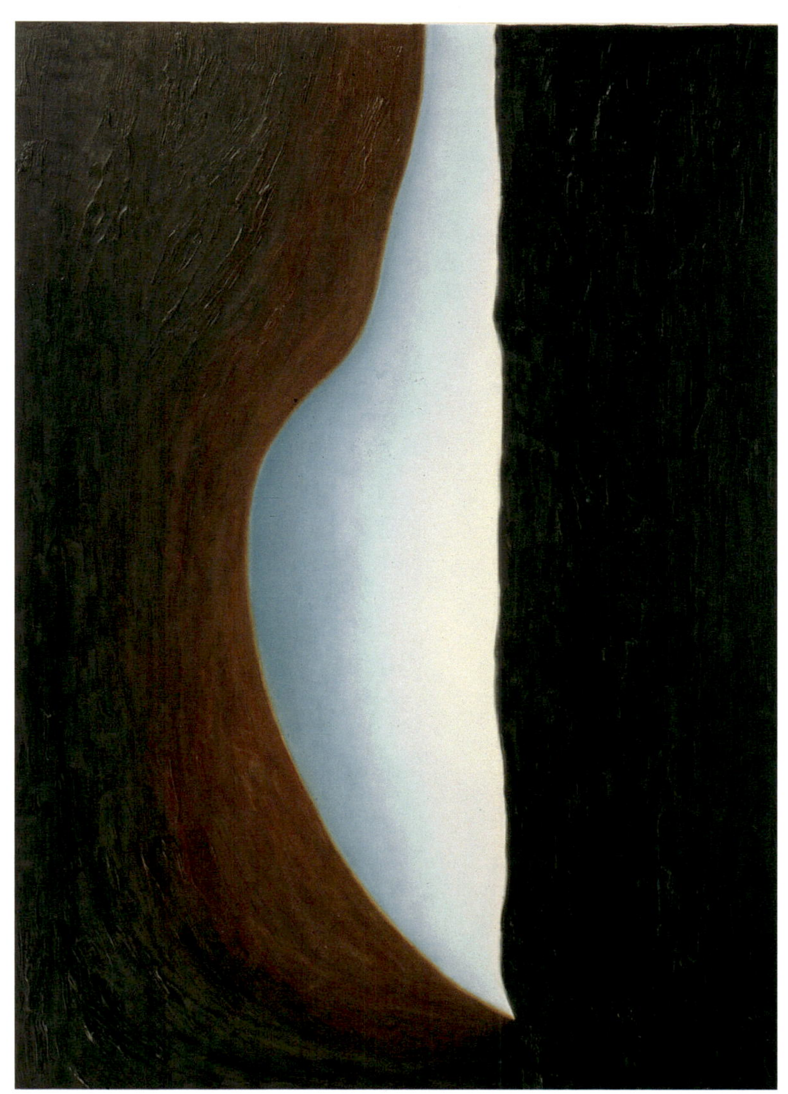

Slot II, 1990, oil stick and oil pastel on paper, 29.5" x 21.5"

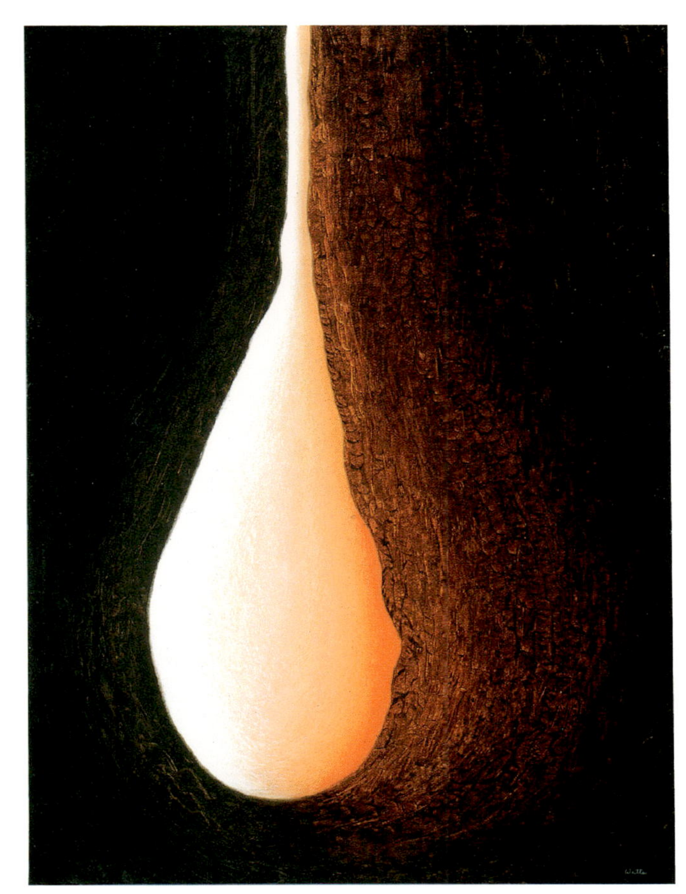

Between, 1990, oil stick and oil pastel on paper, 29.5" x 21.5"

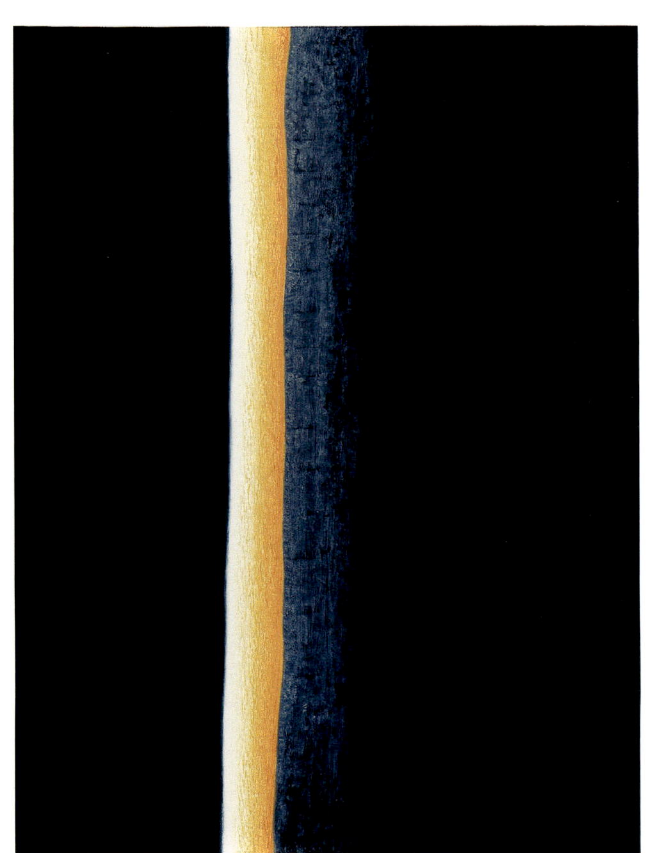

Sipapu 7, 1992, oil stick and oil pastel on paper, 29.5" x 21.5"

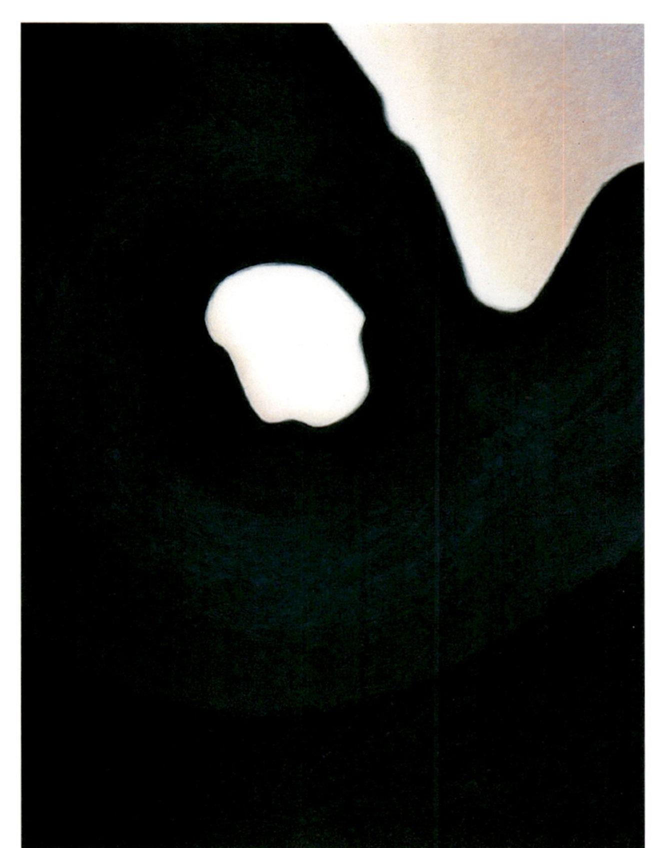

LANDSCAPE 1 SERIES

White Sands, 1988, oil over acrylic on canvas, 42" x 72"

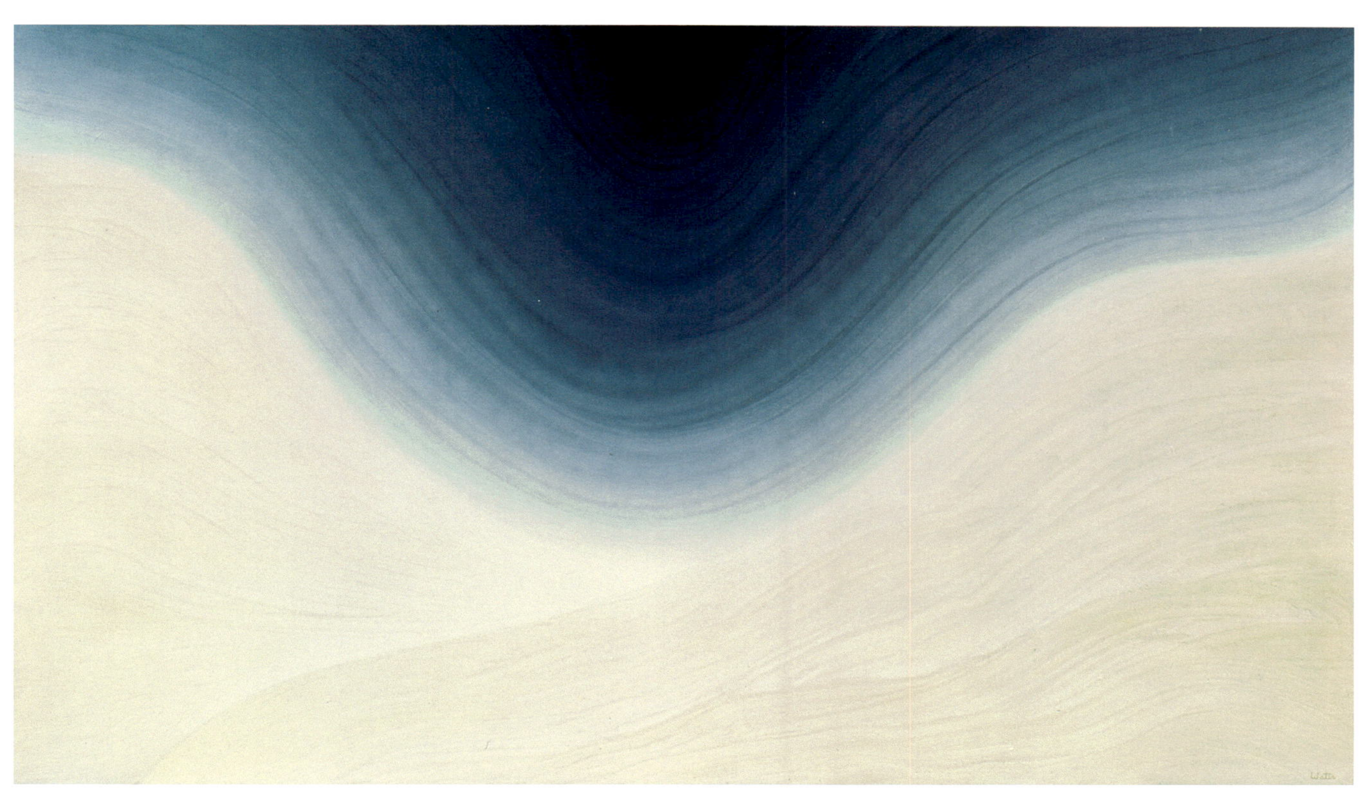

LANDSCAPE 1 SERIES

The Sands, 1988, oil over acrylic on canvas, 36" x 48"

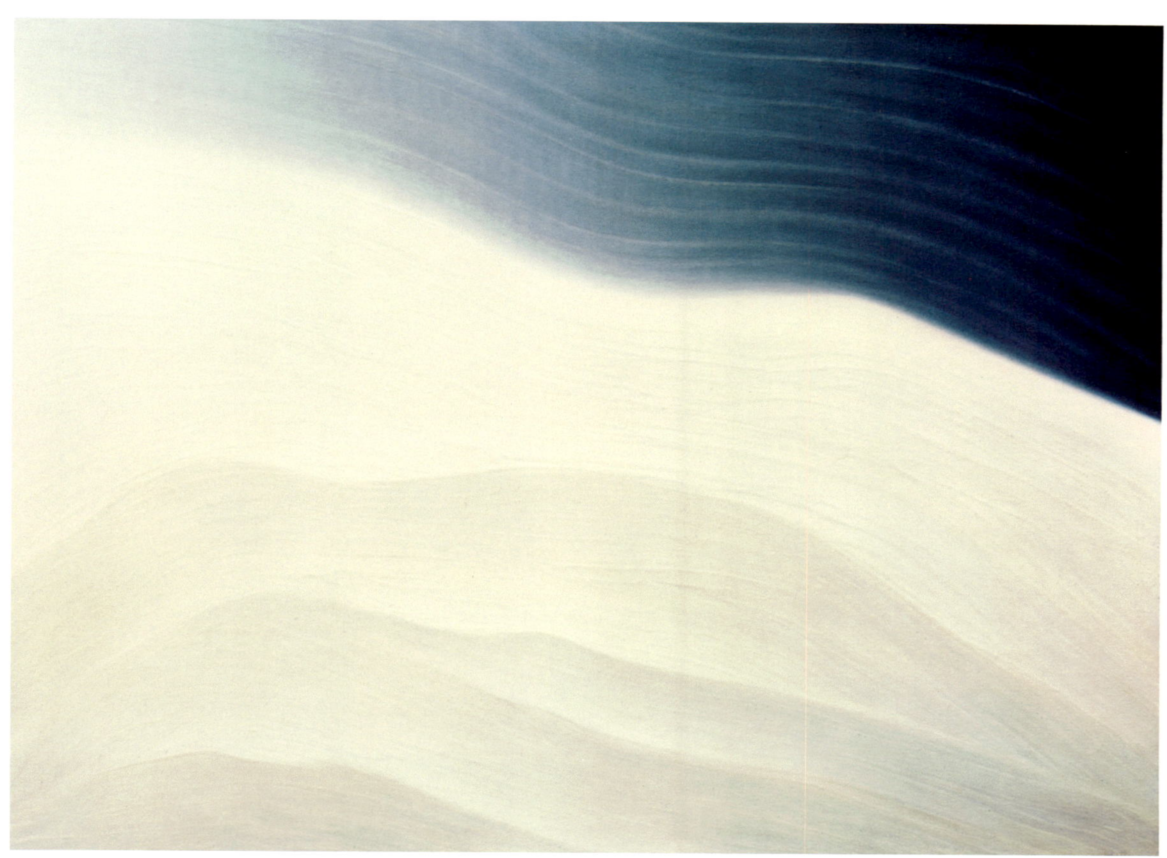

Galisteo IV, 1993, oil on canvas, 48" x 72"

LANDSCAPE 2 SERIES

Union, 1993, oil on canvas, 48" x 72"

LANDSCAPE 2 SERIES

Black, 1993, oil on canvas, 48" x 72"

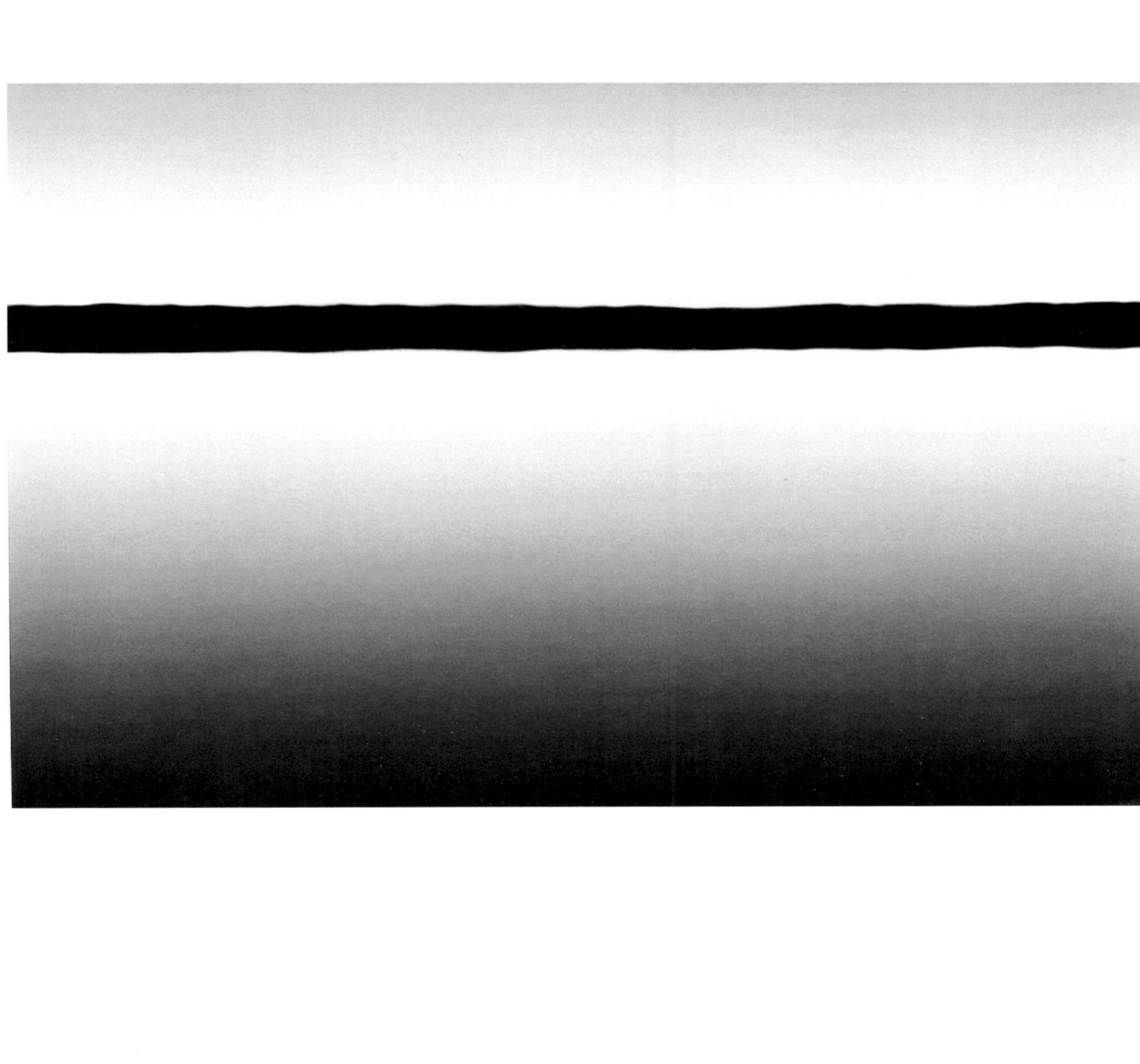

LANDSCAPE 2 SERIES

White, 1993, oil on canvas, 48" x 72"

LANDSCAPE 2 SERIES

Two, 1993, oil on canvas, 48" x 72"

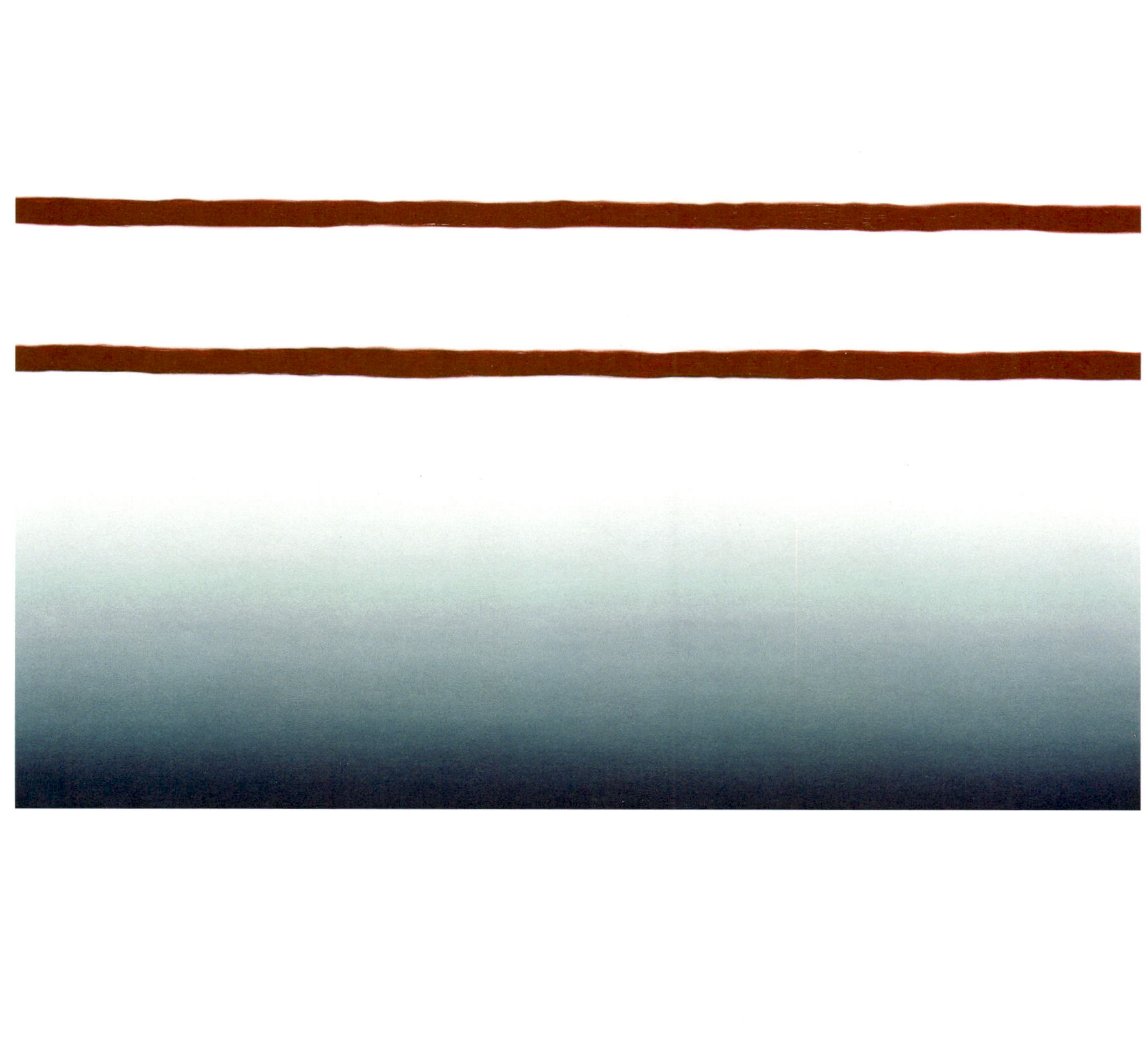

LANDSCAPE 2 SERIES

Prana I, 1993, oil on canvas, 48" x 72"

LANDSCAPE 2 SERIES

La Luz, 1993, oil on canvas, 48" x 72"

ZAZEN SERIES

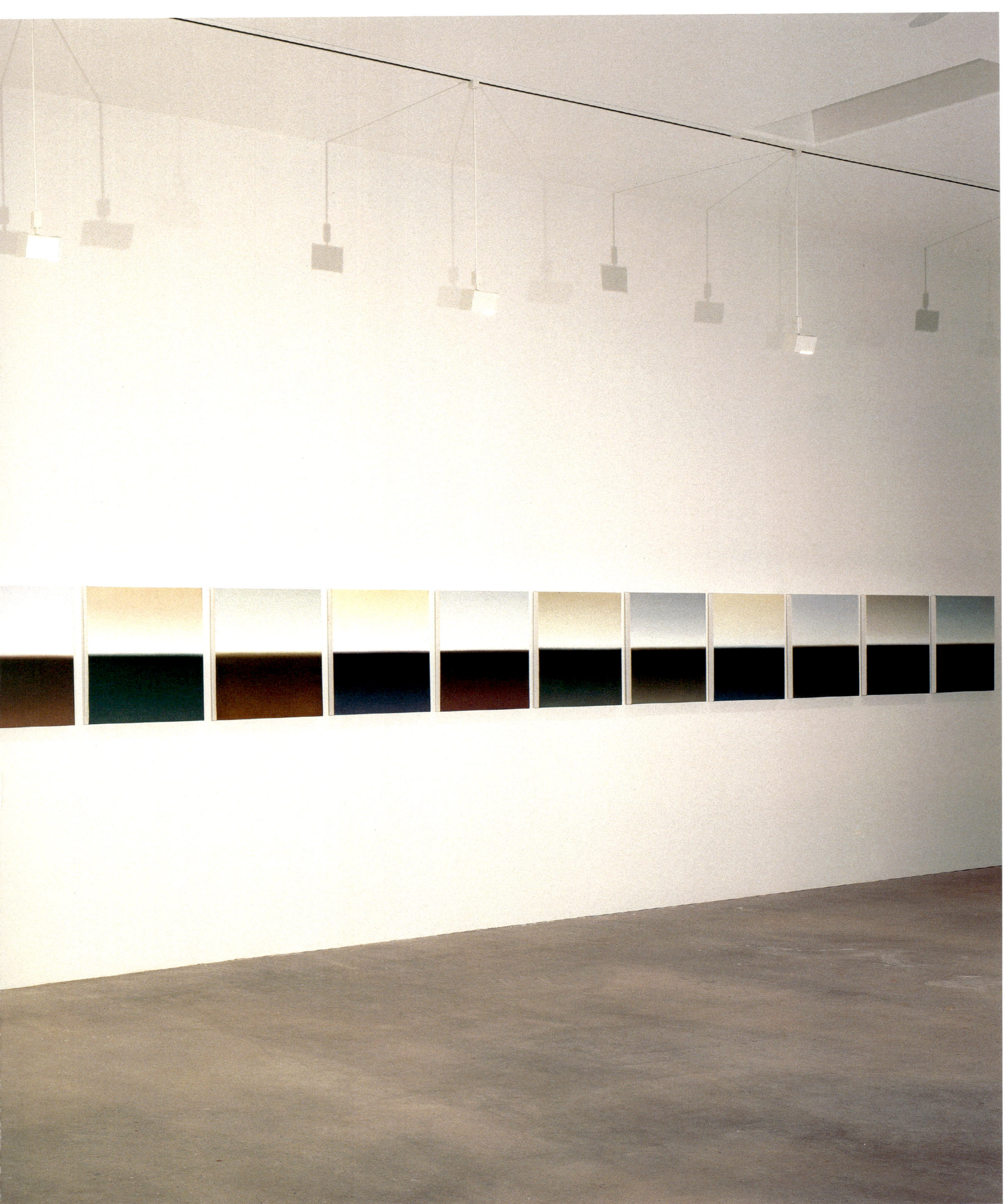

Installation View, Artist's Studio, 1995

ZAZEN SERIES

Zazen 1, 1995, oil on canvas, 26" x 26"

ZAZEN SERIES

Zazen 2, 1995, oil on canvas, 26" x 26"

ZAZEN SERIES

Zazen 3, 1995, oil on canvas, 26" x 26"

ZAZEN SERIES

Triptych, 1995, oil on canvas, 26" x 80"

ZAZEN SERIES

Light III, 1995, oil on canvas, 28" x 28"

GEOMETRIC SERIES

Three, 1995, oil on canvas, 24" x 80"

GEOMETRIC SERIES

Yantra VI, 1996, oil on canvas, 24" x 24"

GEOMETRIC SERIES

X-I, 1995, oil on canvas, 30" x 30"

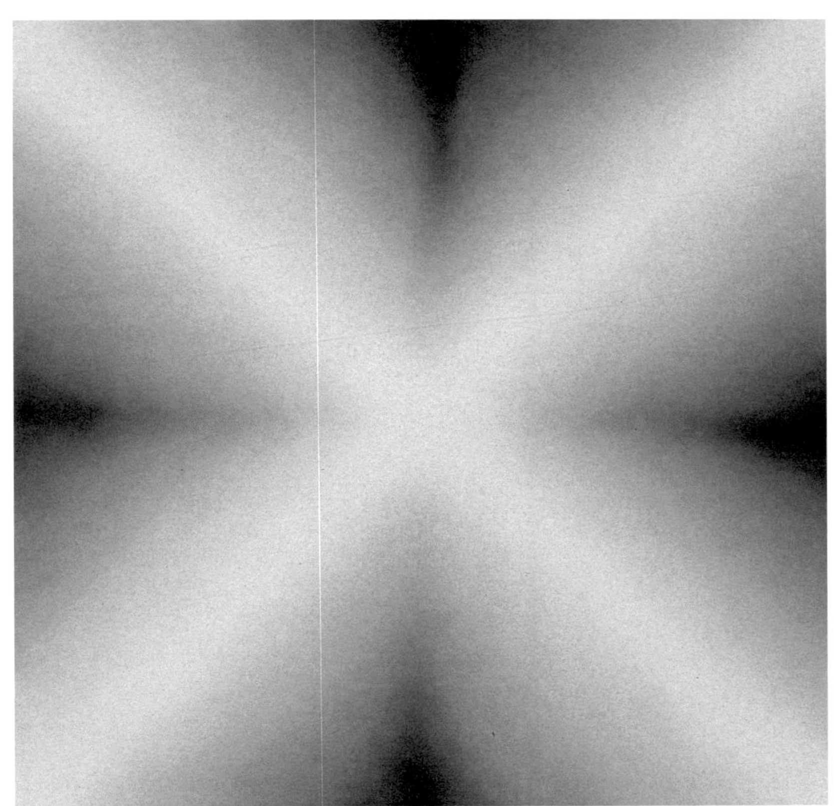

Yantra V, 1996, oil on canvas, 24" x 24"

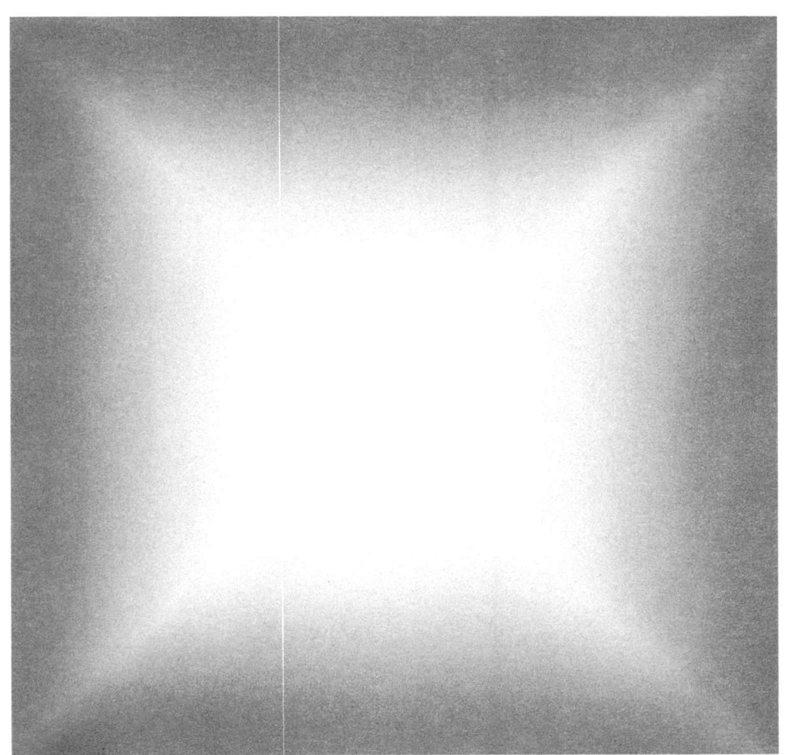

GEOMETRIC SERIES

Yantra III, 1996, oil on canvas, 24" x 24"

GEOMETRIC SERIES

X-II, 1995, oil on canvas, 30" x 30"

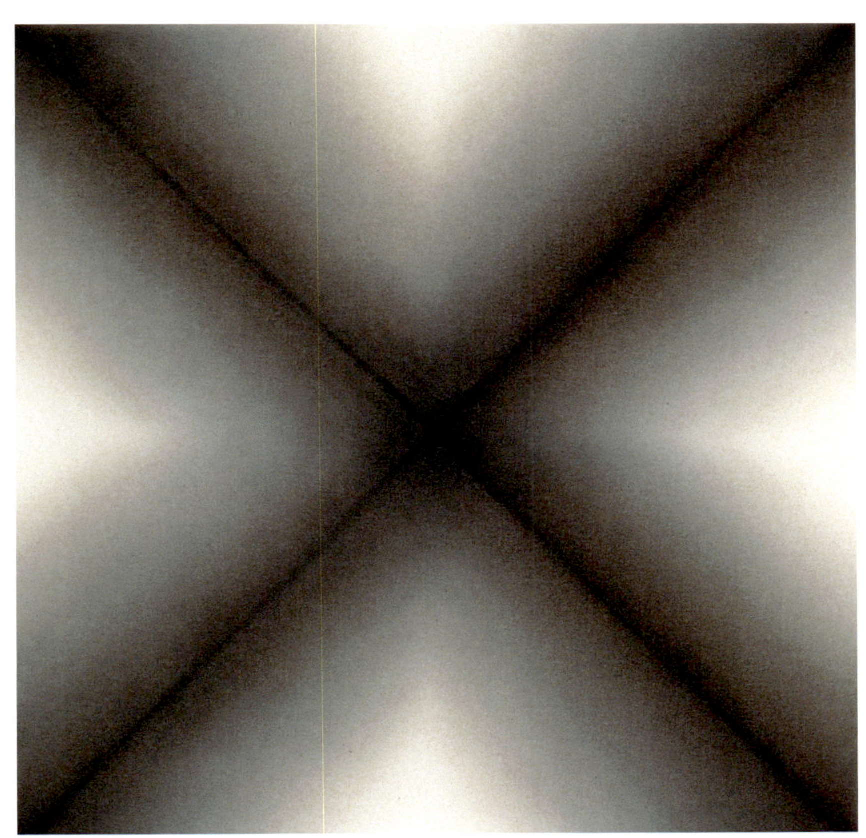

GEOMETRIC SERIES

Duo, 1996, oil on canvas, 24" x 24" each panel

WHITE SERIES

Beyond XII, 1998, oil on canvas, 30" x 30"

Beyond XVI, 1999, oil on canvas, 42" x 42"

WHITE SERIES

Beyond IXV, 1999, oil on canvas, 48" x 48"

WHITE SERIES

Open XIV, 2000, oil on canvas, 30" x 30"

WHITE SERIES

Open VI, 2000, oil on canvas, 60" x 30"

WHITE SERIES

Open XII, 2000, oil on canvas, 68" x 34"

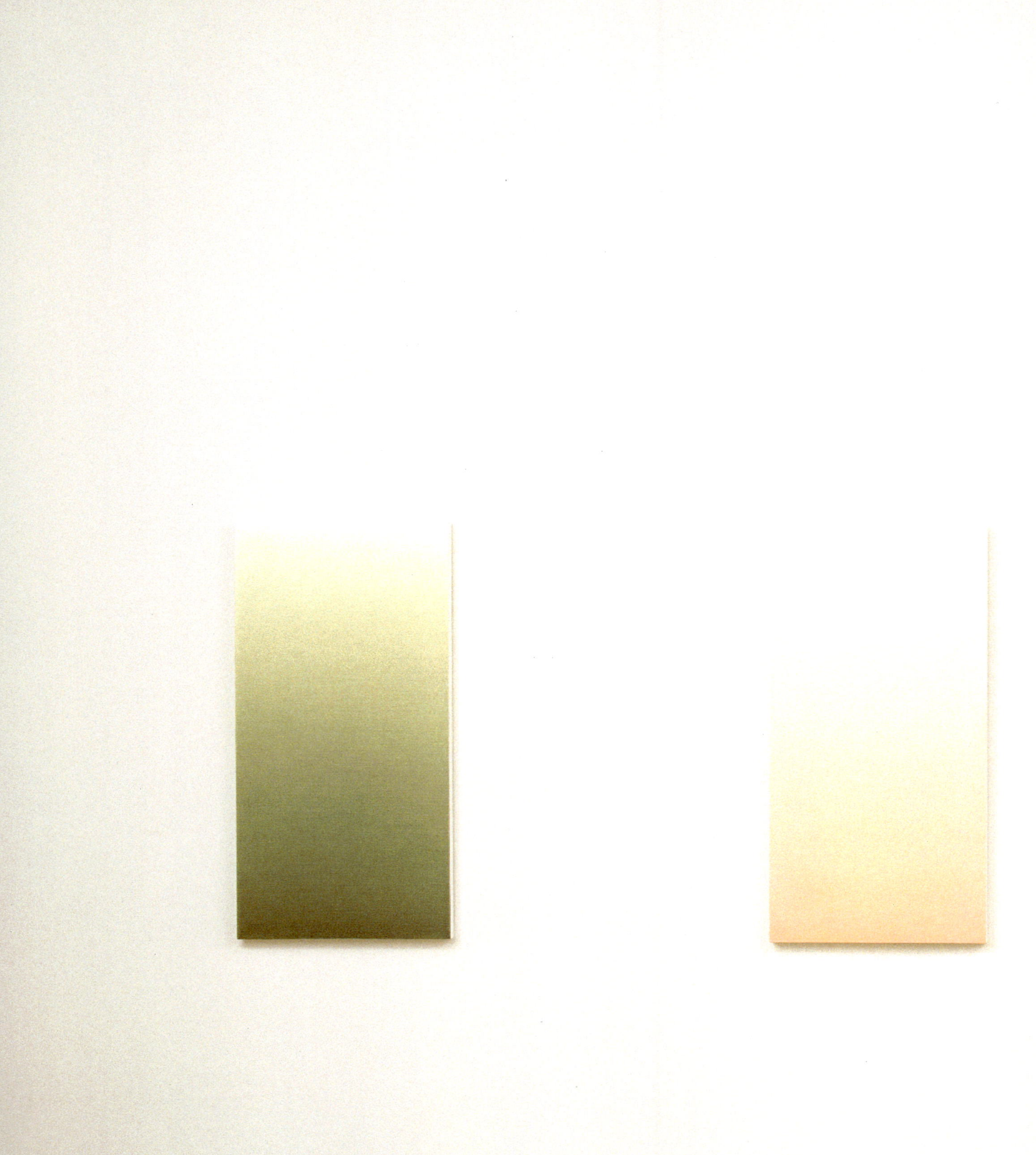

Installation View, Artist's Studio, 2002, photo: Herb Lotz

0-38, 2003, oil on canvas, 44" x 22"

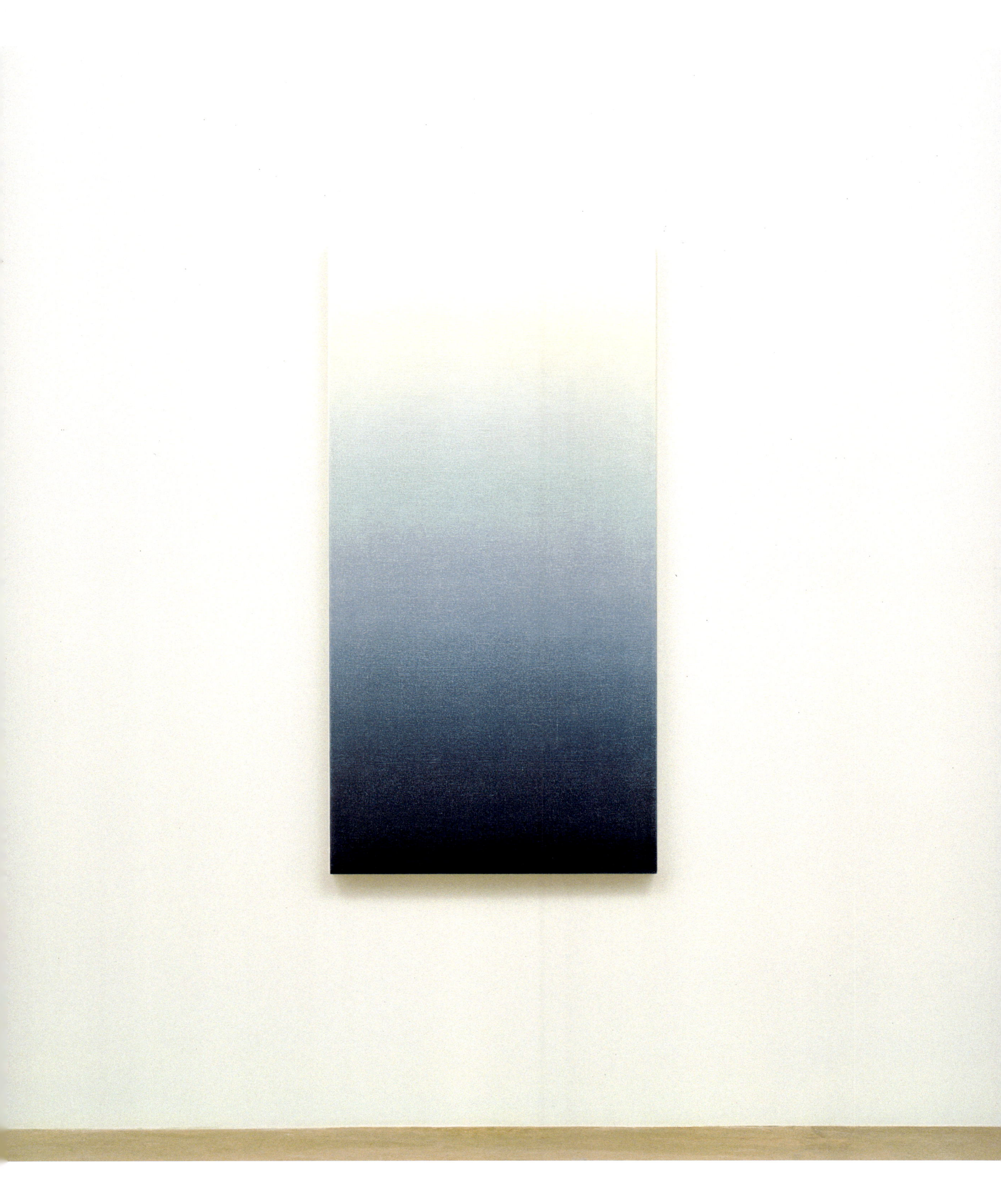

SERIES ZERO

0-1, 2002, oil on canvas, 44" x 22"

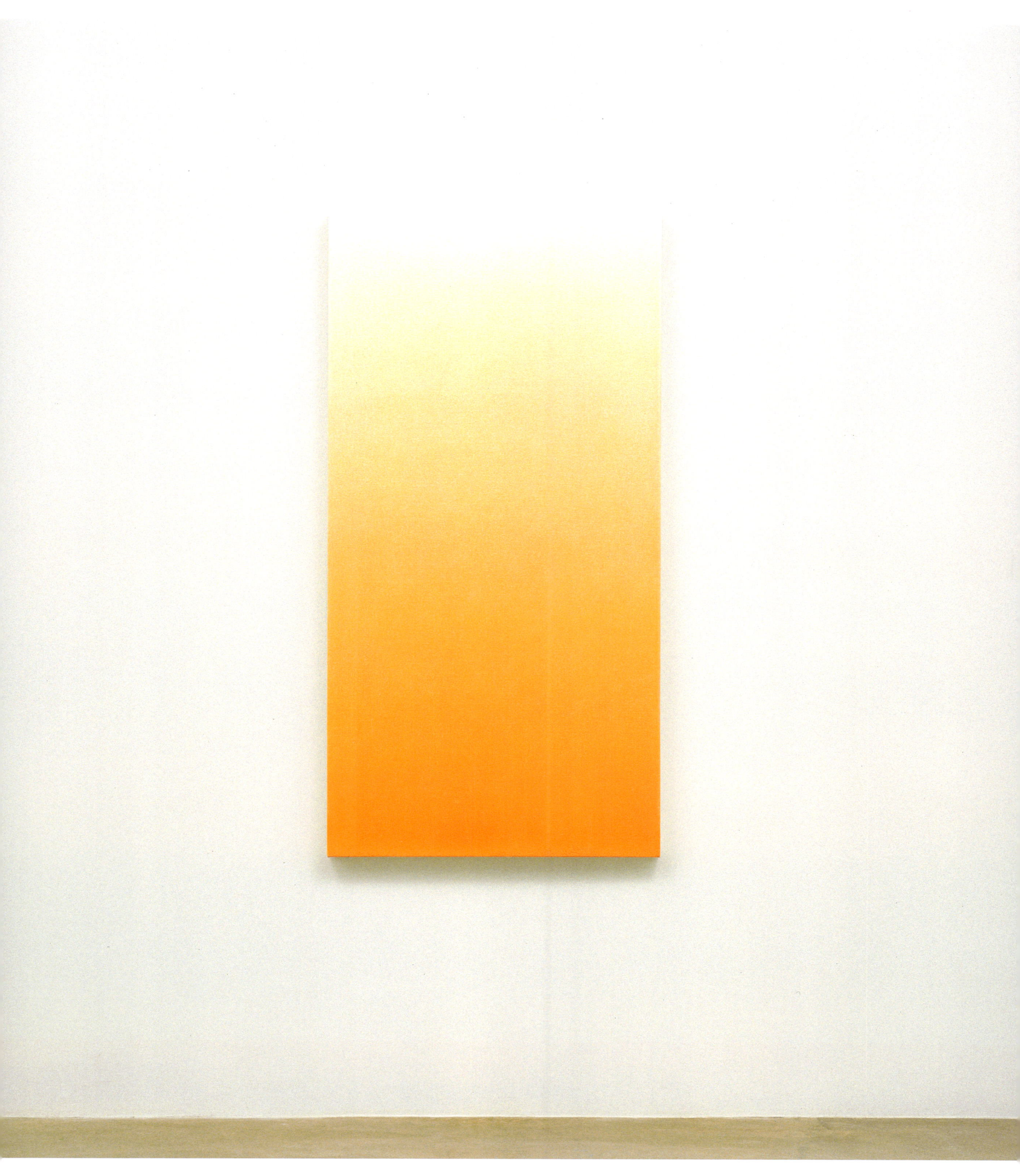

0-21, 2002, oil on canvas, 44" x 22"

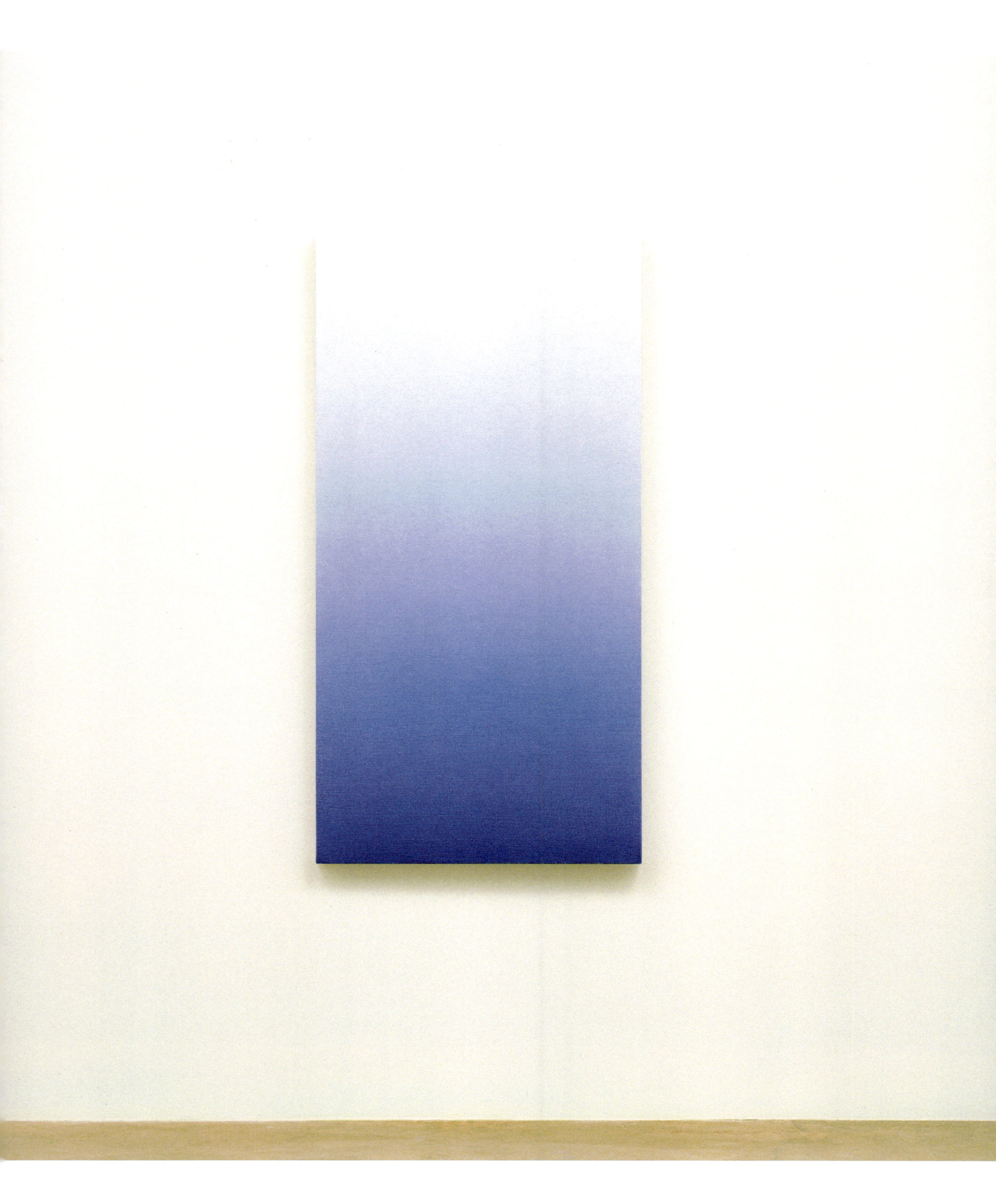

SERIES ZERO

0-6, 2002, oil on canvas, 44" x 22"

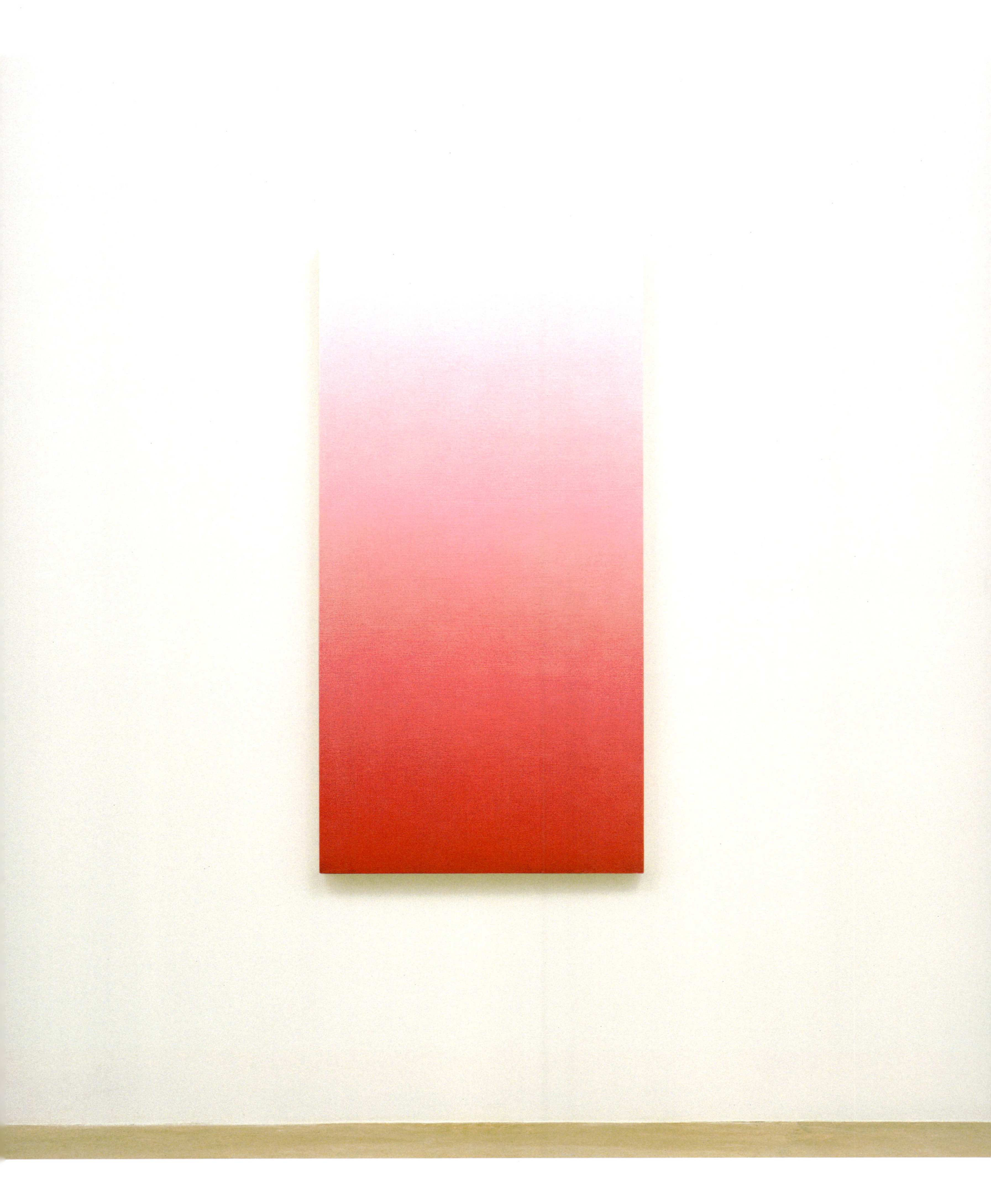

SERIES ZERO

0-28, 2003, oil on canvas, 44" x 22"

0-26, 2003, oil on canvas, 44" x 22"

SERIES ZERO

0-34, 2003, oil on canvas, 44" x 22"

0-23, 2003, oil on canvas, 44" x 22"

SERIES THREE

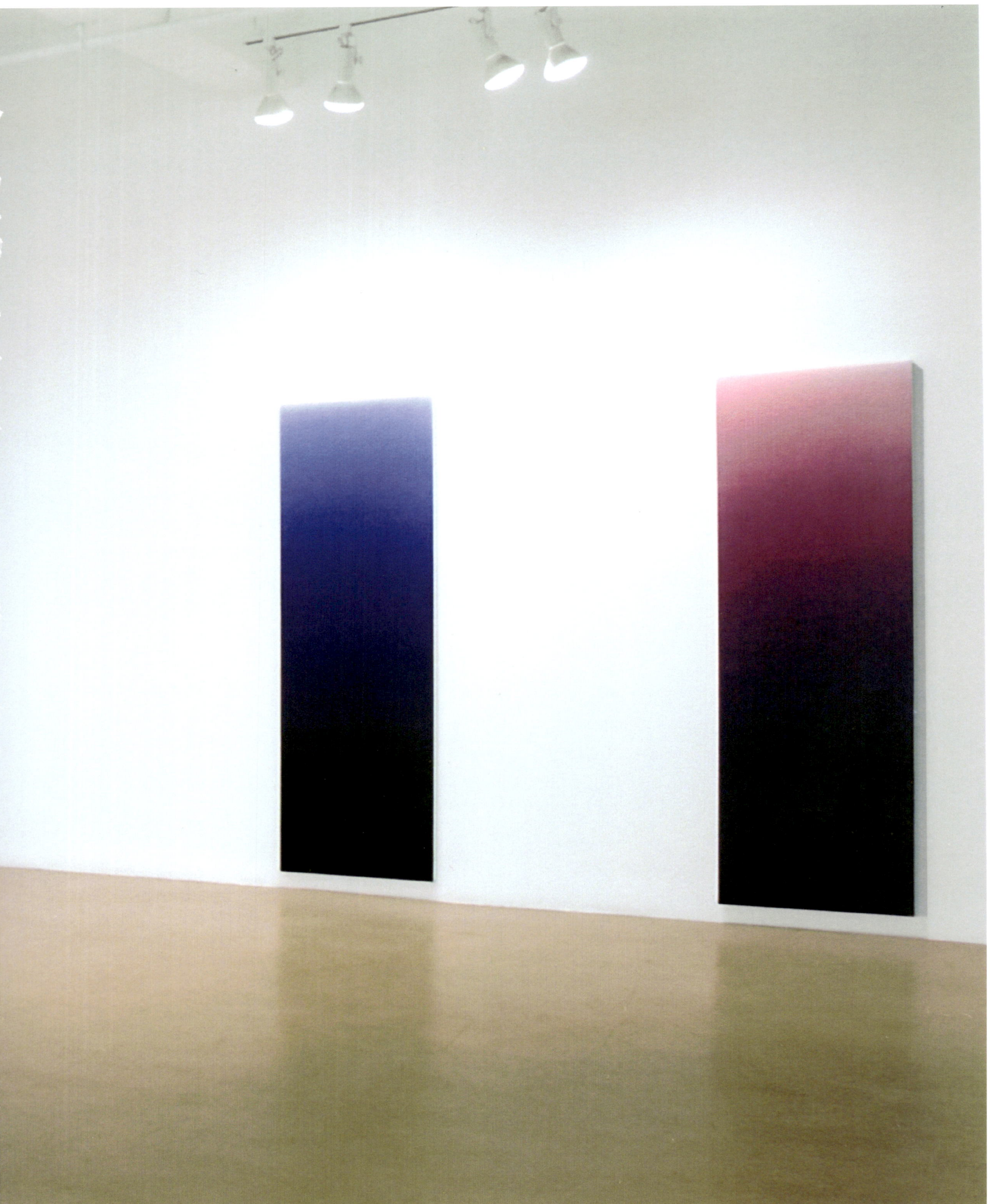

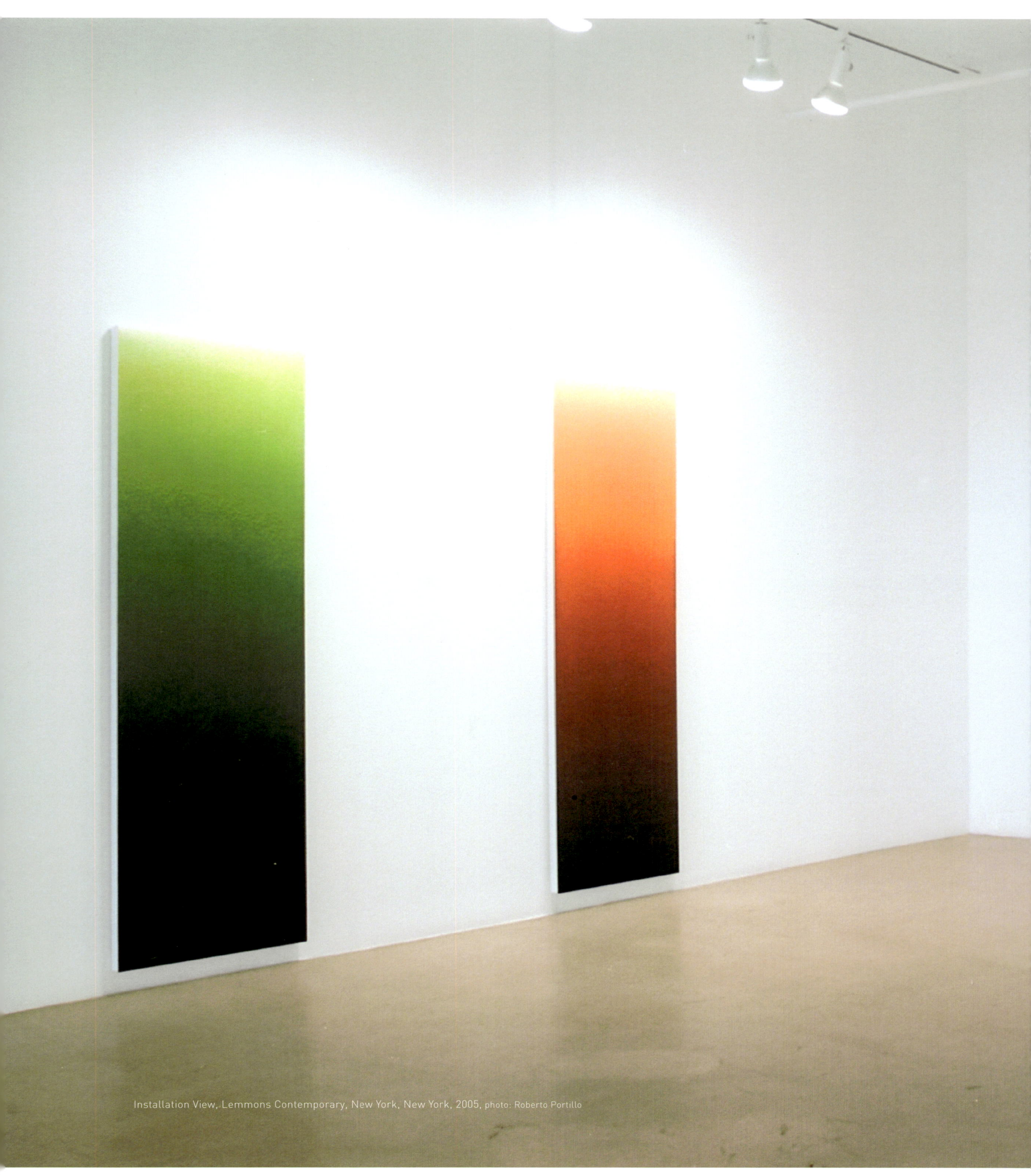
Installation View, Lemmons Contemporary, New York, New York, 2005, photo: Roberto Portillo

III-3, 2004, oil on canvas, 72" x 24"

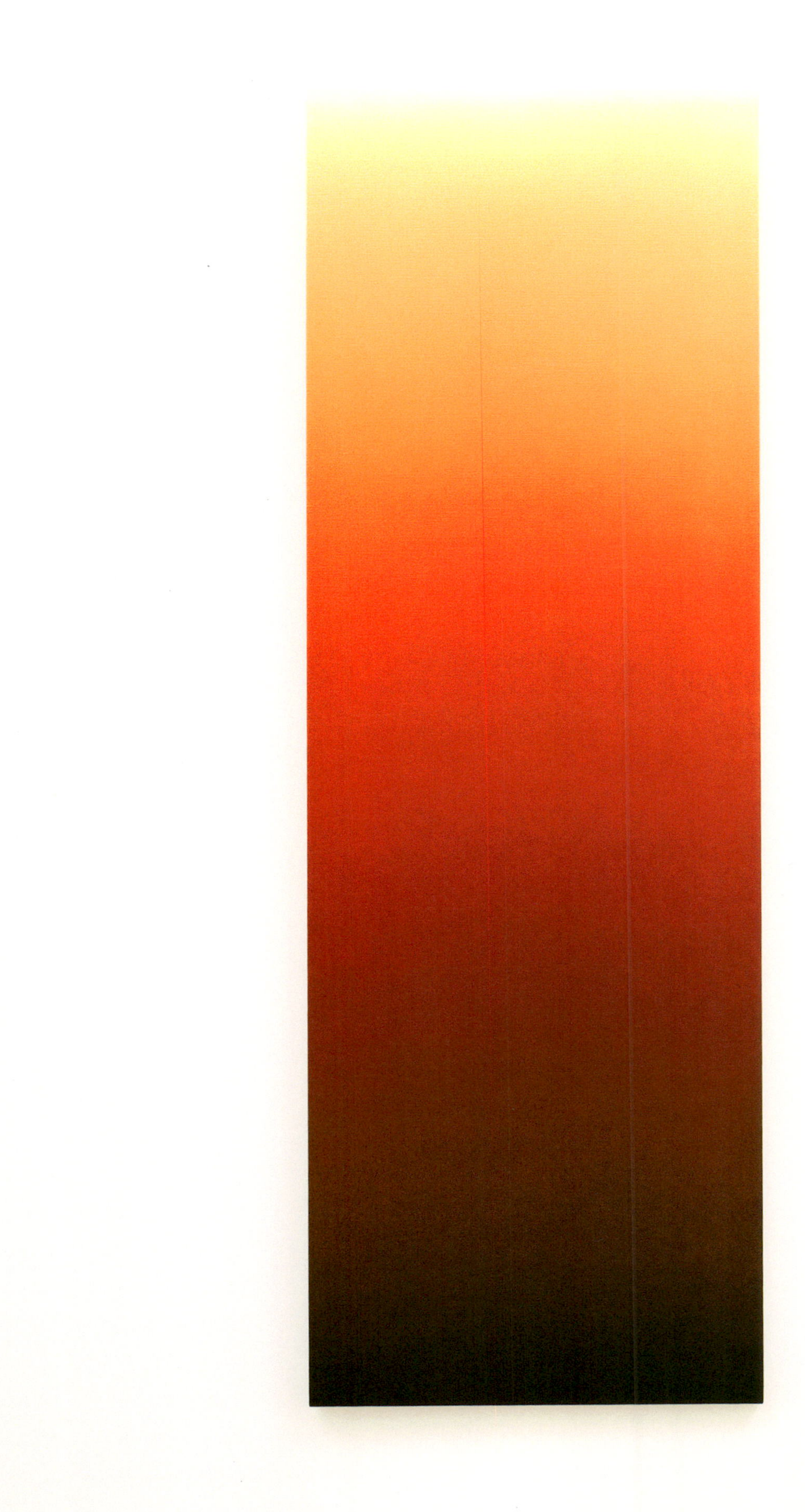

SERIES THREE

III-4, 2005, oil on canvas, 72" x 24"

SERIES THREE

III-1, 2005, oil on canvas, 72" x 24"

SERIES THREE

III-2, 2004, oil on canvas, 72" x 24"

SERIES THREE

Two I-II, 2004, oil on canvas, 22" x 111.5"

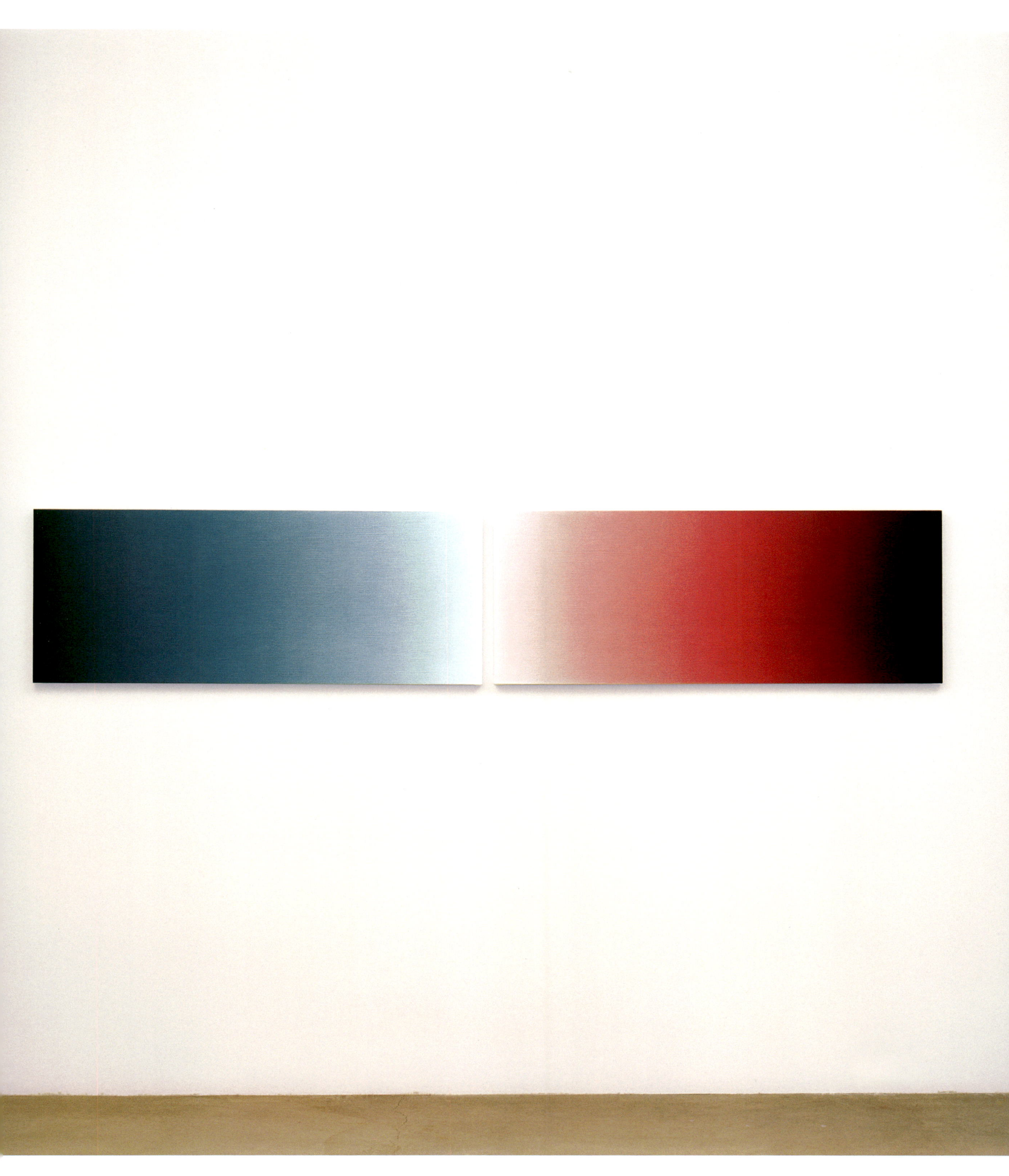

SERIES THREE

III-5 and **III-6,** 2004, oil on canvas, 72" x 24" each

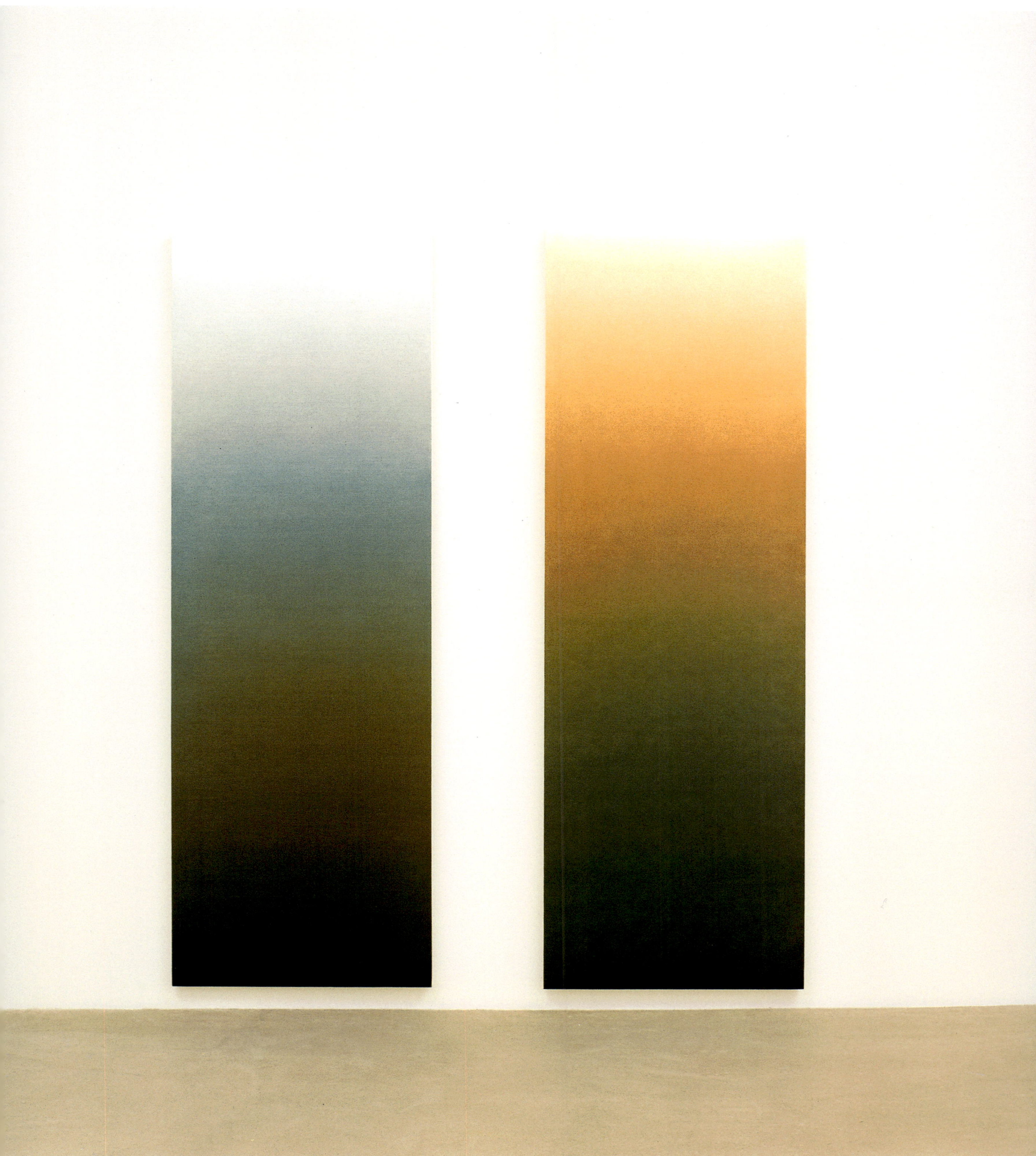

SERIES THREE

Suite, 2005, oil on canvas, 72" x 144"

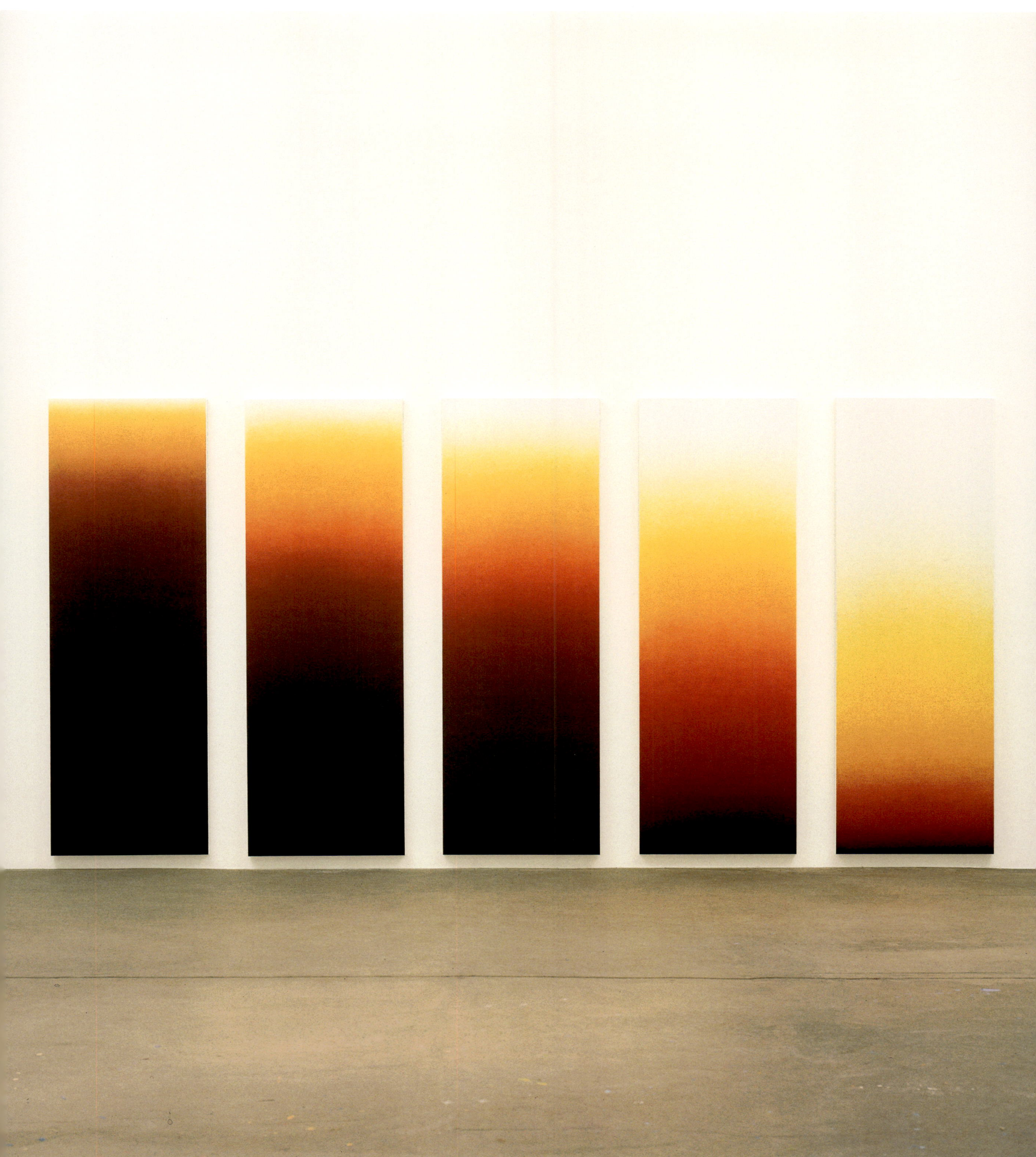

SERIES X

X-II, 2006, oil on canvas, 72" x 24"

SERIES X

X-13, 2006, oil on canvas, 72" x 24"

SERIES X

X-16, 2006, oil on canvas, 24" x 72"

SERIES X

X-17, 2006, oil on canvas, 72" x 24"

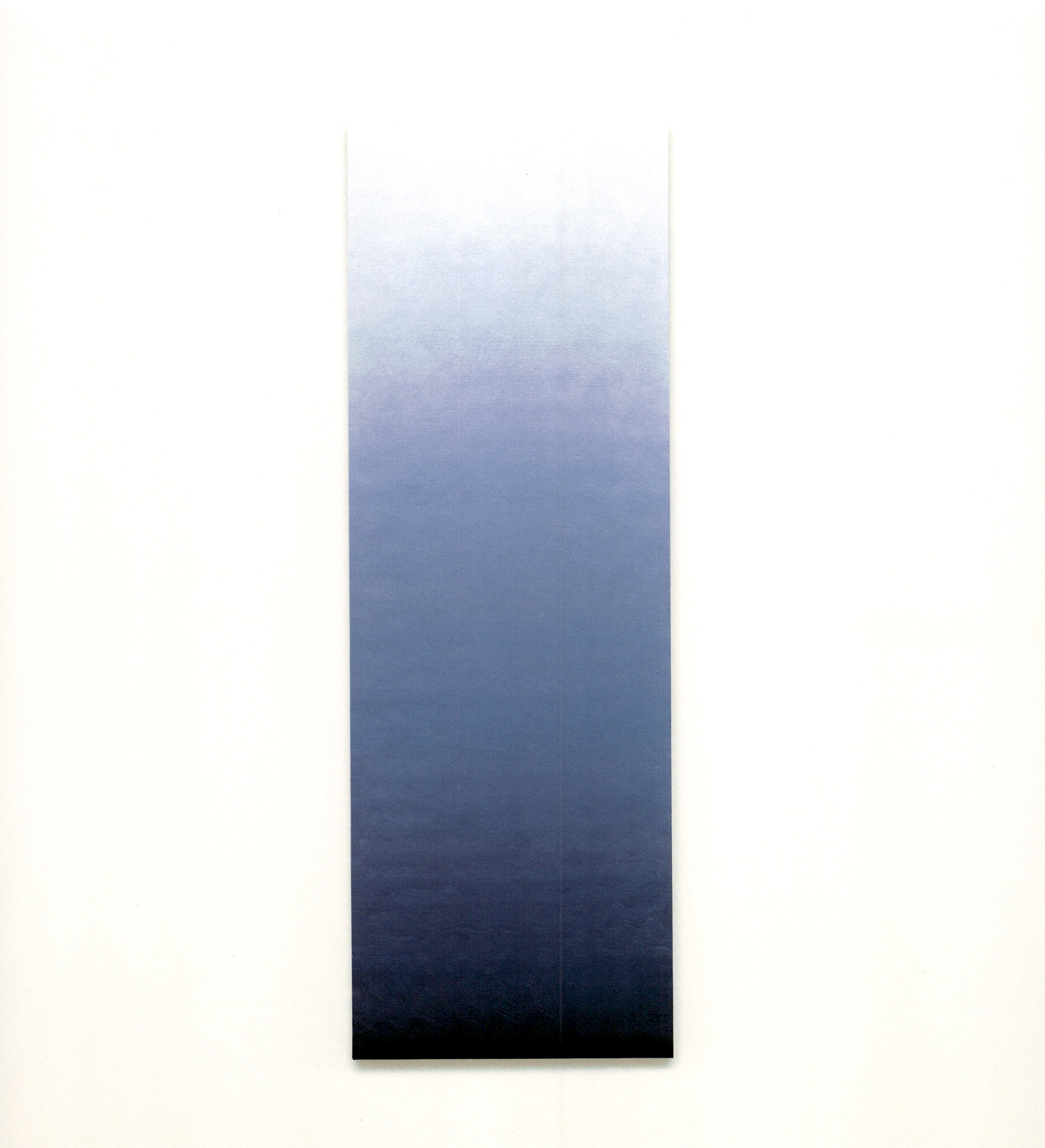

SERIES X

X-10, 2006, oil on canvas, 72" x 24"

SERIES X

X-14, 2006, oil on canvas, 72" x 24"

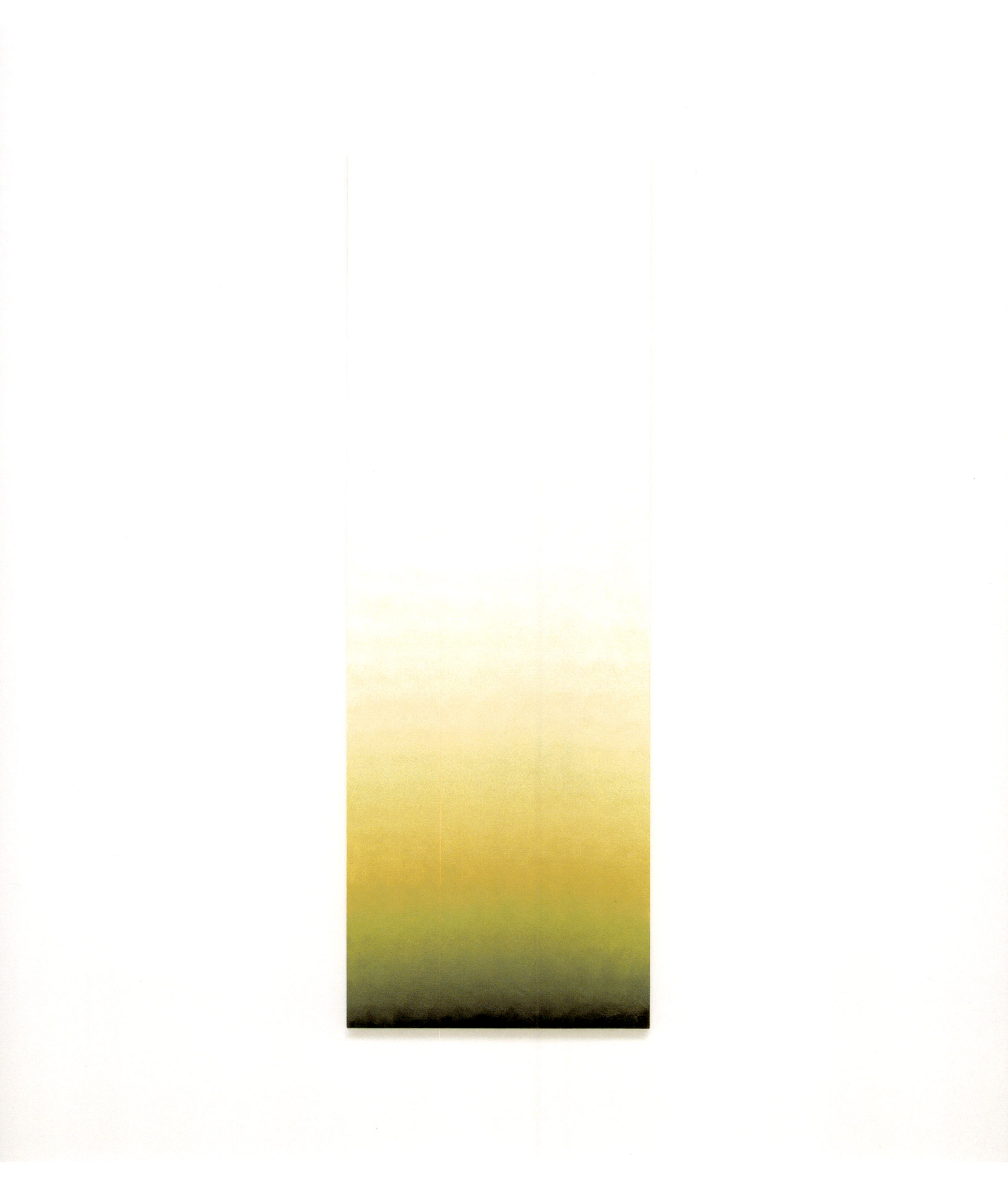

X-8, 2006, oil on canvas, 24" x 72"

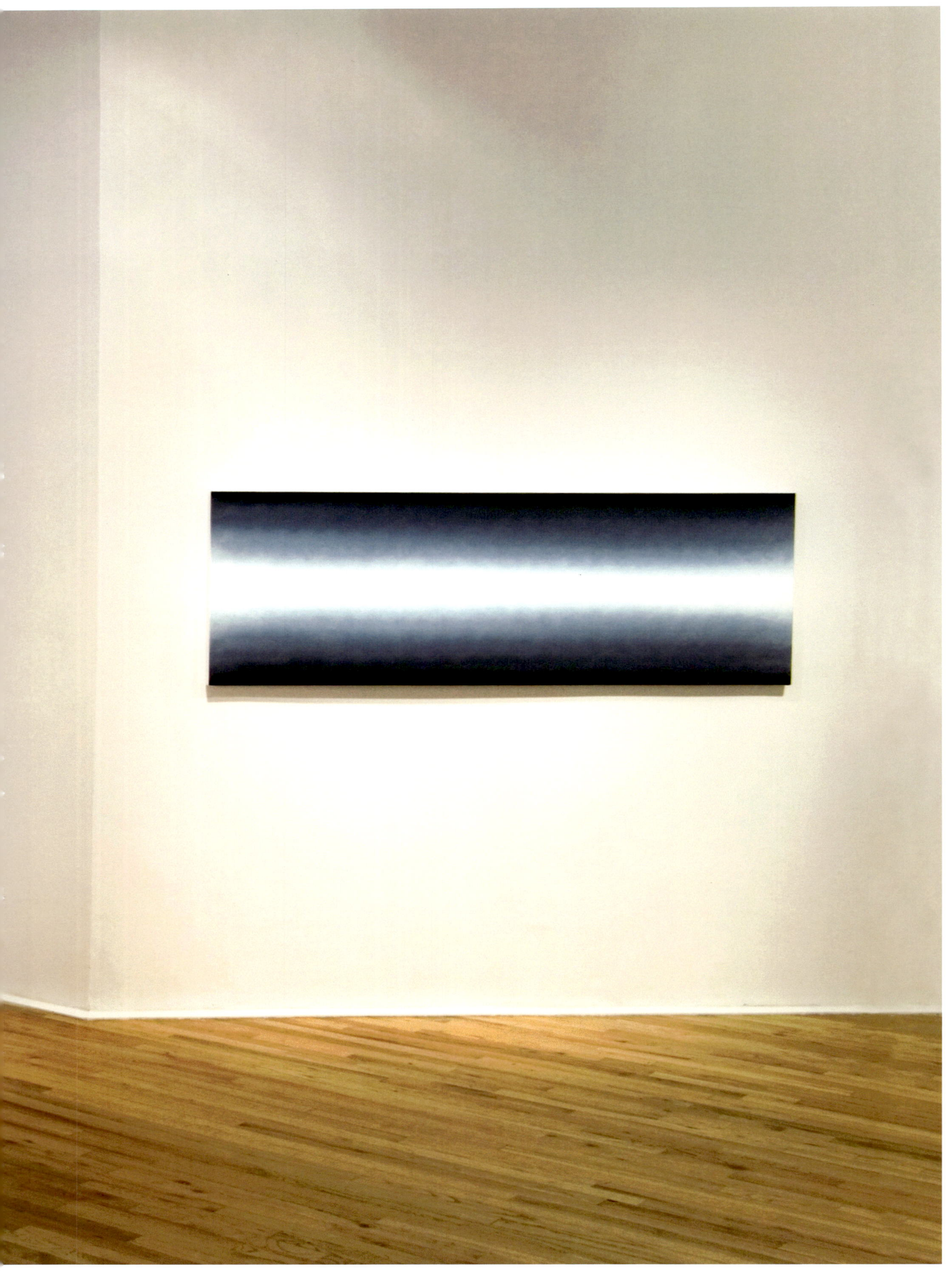

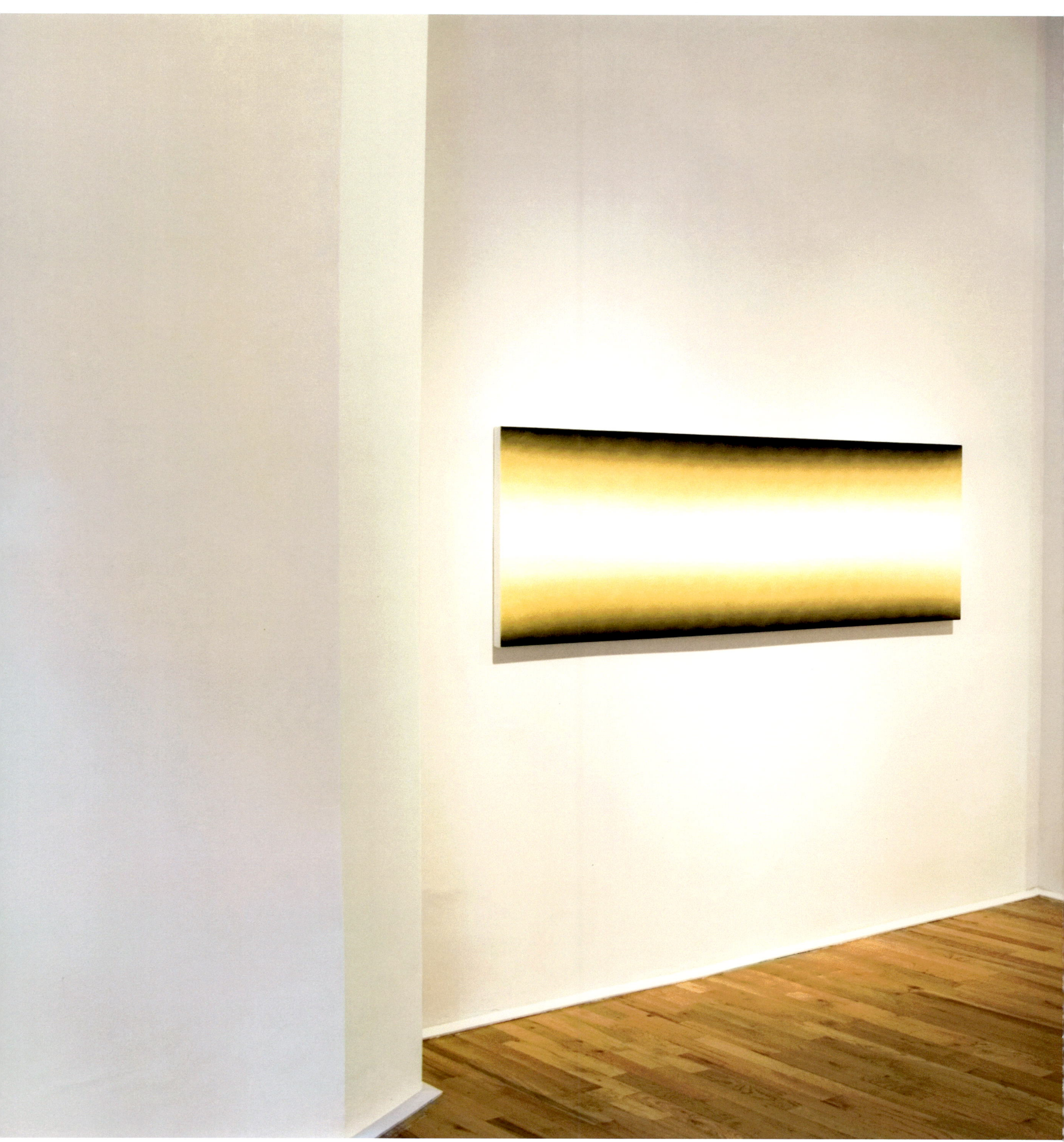

Installation View, Lemmons Contemporary, New York, New York, 2007, photo: Roberto Portillo

Channel 3, 2007, oil on canvas, 24" x 72"

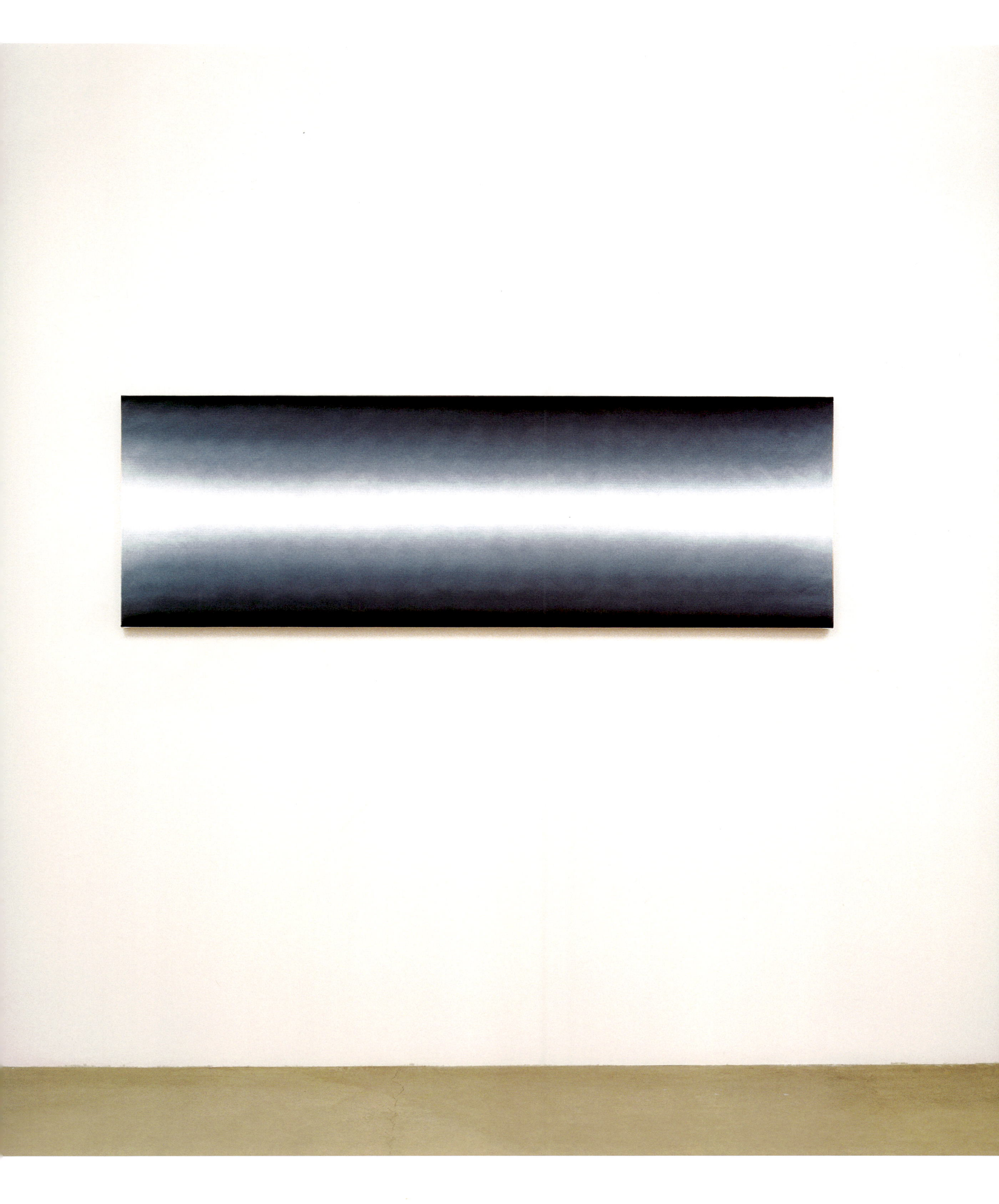

Channel 4, 2007, oil on canvas, 24" x 72"

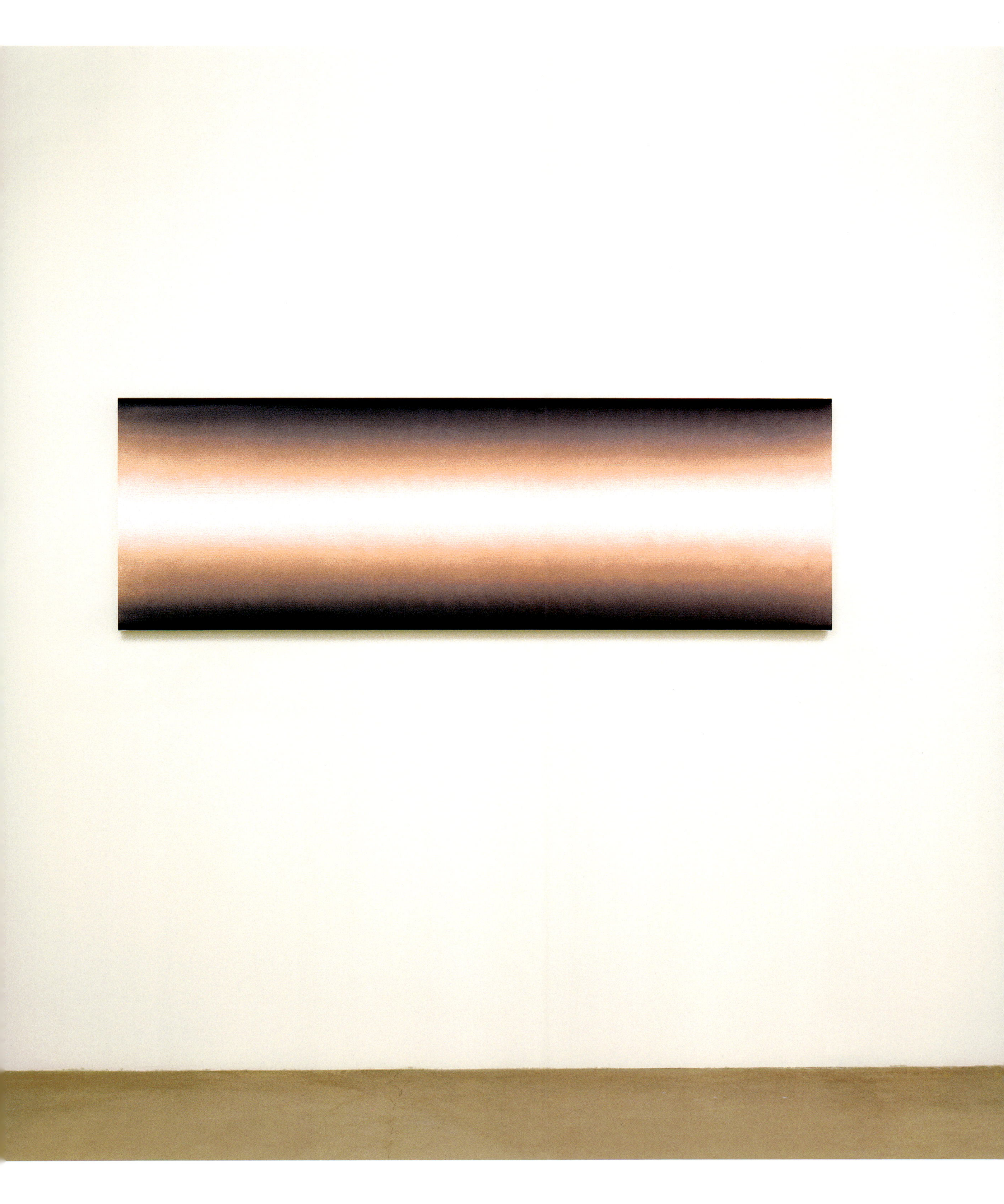

CHANNEL SERIES

Channel 2, 2007, oil on canvas, 24" x 72"

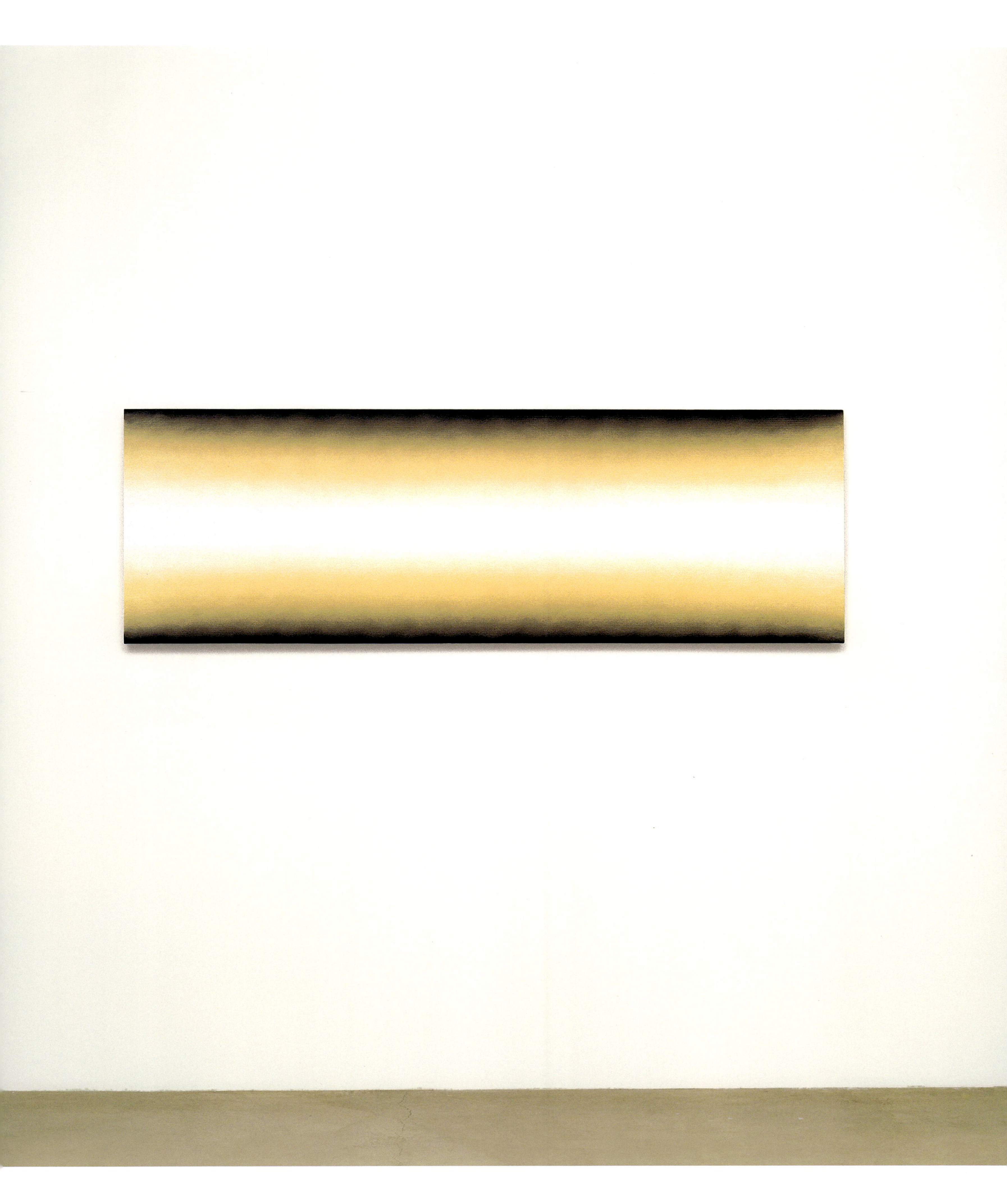

CHANNEL SERIES

Channel 5, 2007, oil on canvas, 24" x 72"

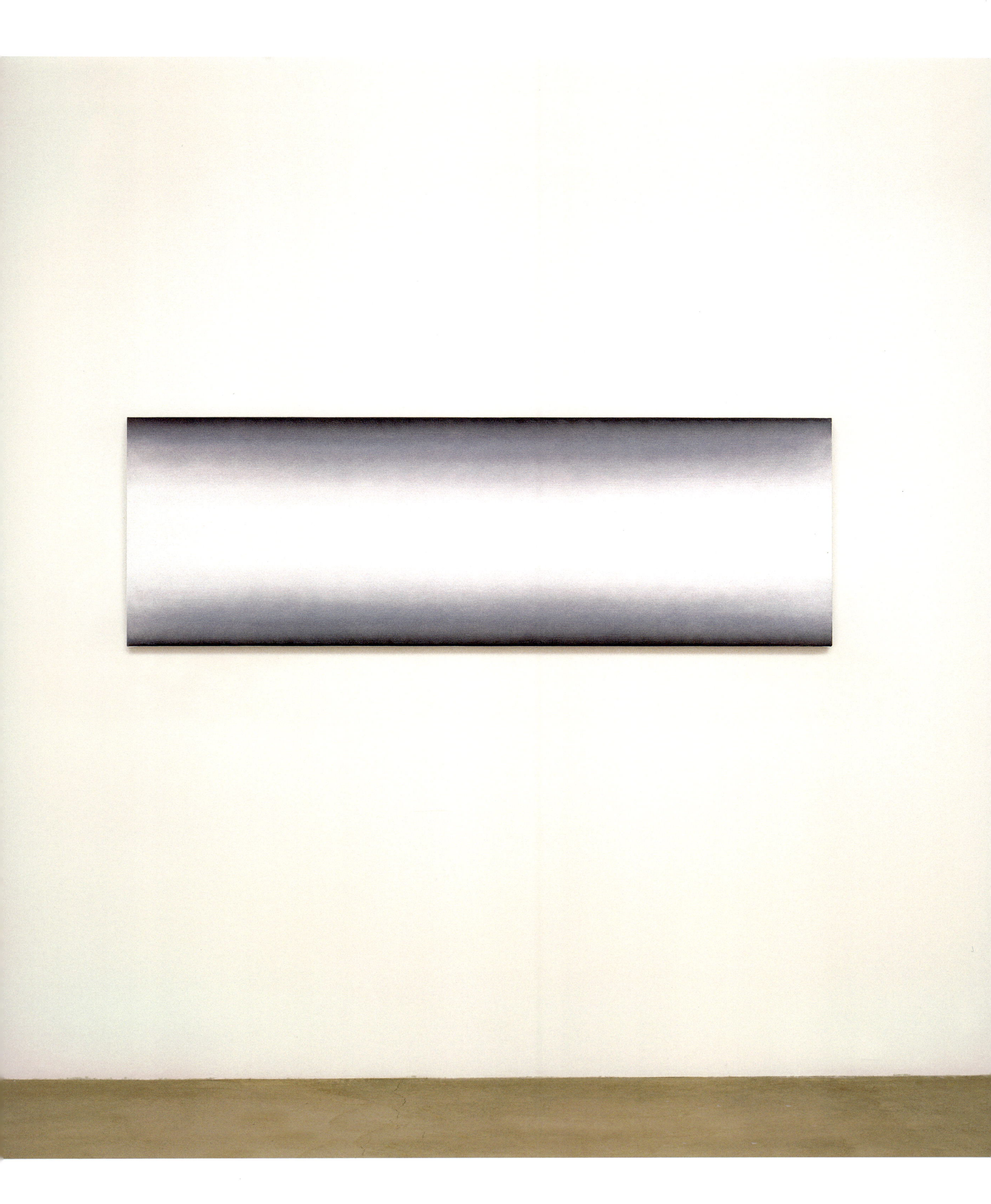

Channel 9, 2007, oil on canvas, 36" x 72"

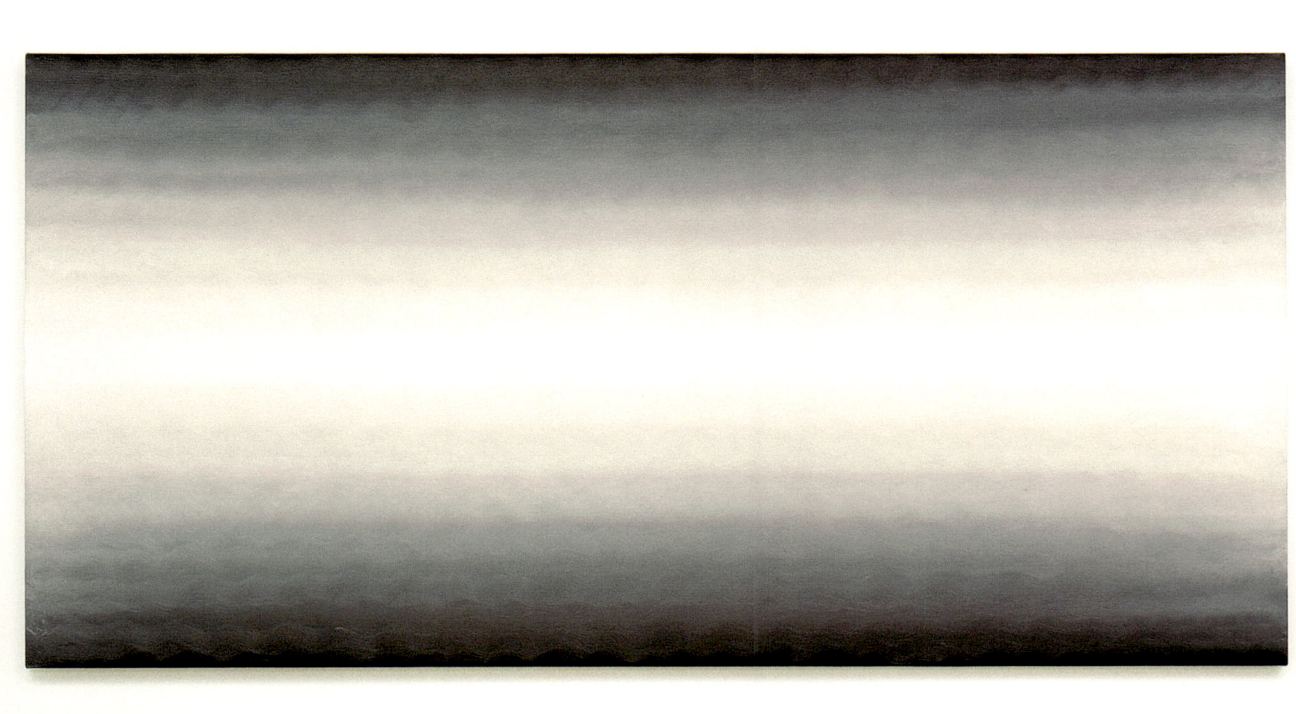

Channel 8, 2007, oil on canvas, 36" x 72"

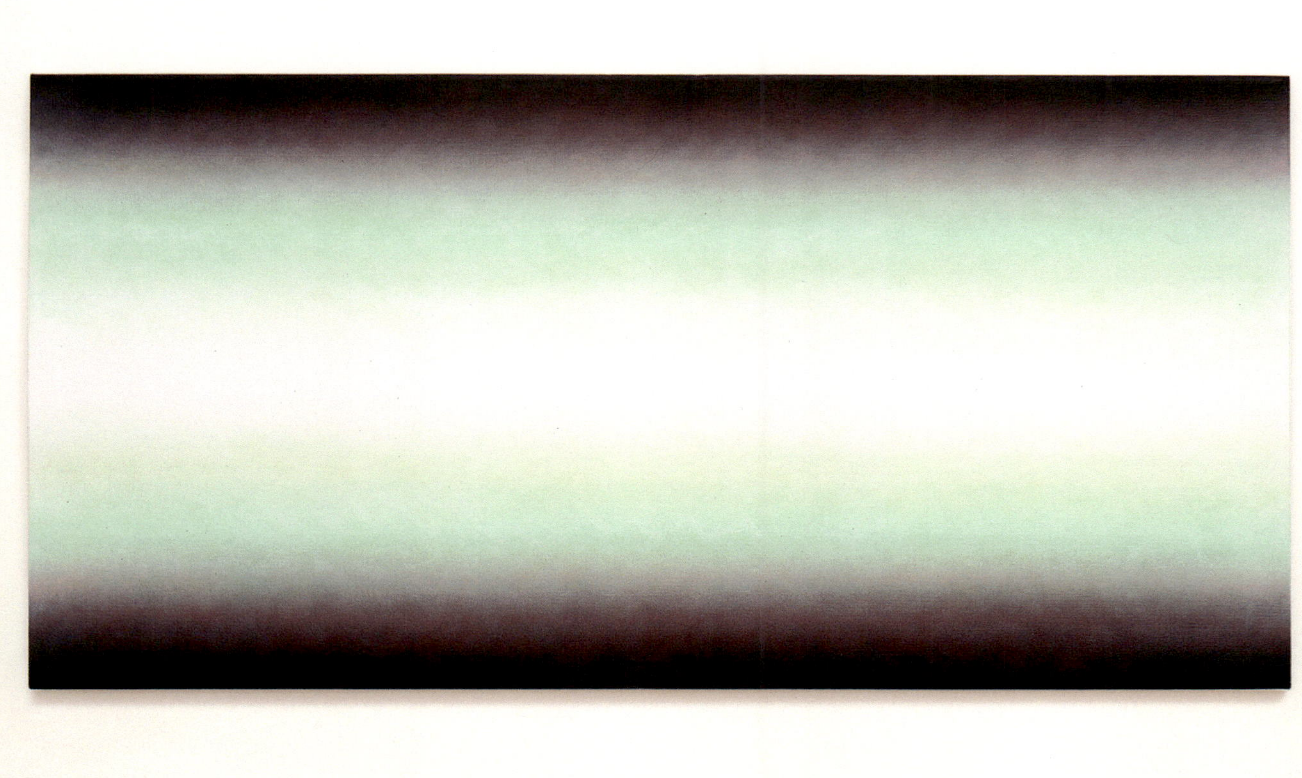

Channel 10, 2007, oil on canvas, 30" x 90"

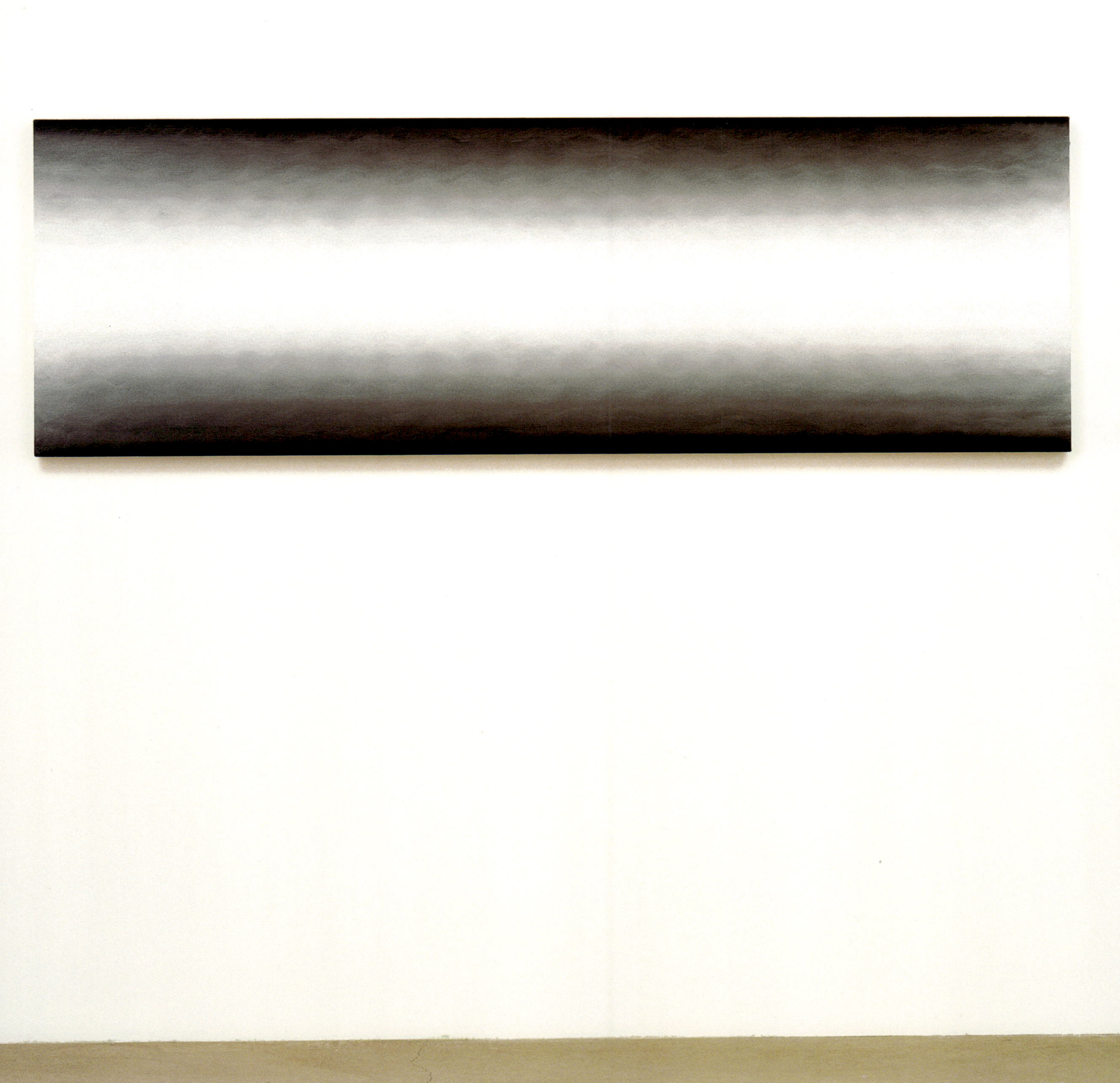

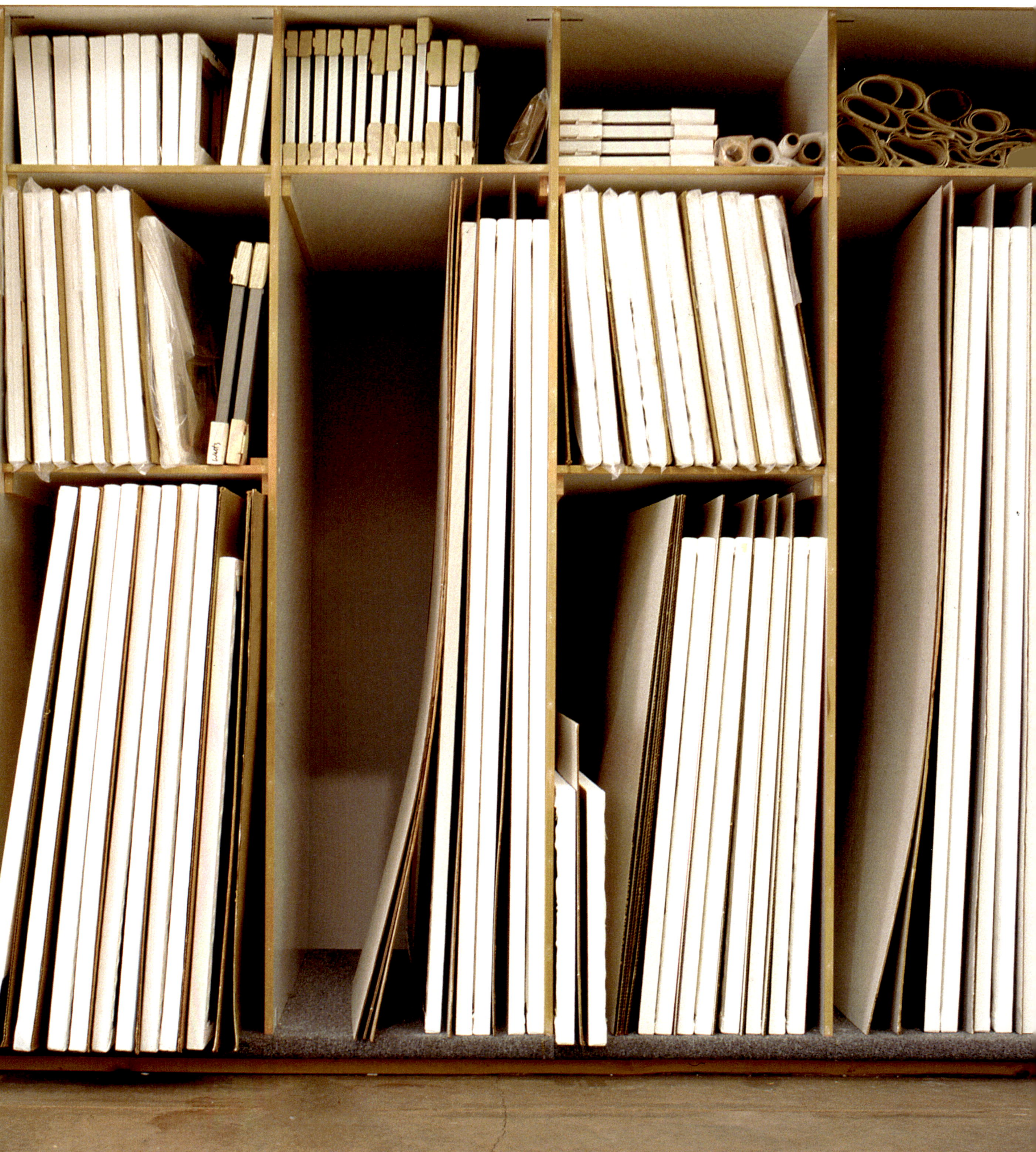

left: Artist's studio, 2008
photo: Herb Lotz

Solo Exhibitions

2008	Charlotte Jackson Fine Art, Santa Fe, New Mexico
2007	Lemmons Contemporary, New York, New York
2005	Lemmons Contemporary, New York, New York
2000	Charlotte Jackson Fine Art, Santa Fe, New Mexico
1998	Whelan Gallery, Santa Fe, New Mexico
1996	Galerie Ulrike Buschlinger, Wiesbaden, Germany
1994	Santuario de Guadalupe, Santa Fe, New Mexico
1993	Spirit Gallery, Santa Fe, New Mexico
1992	Peyton-Wright Galleries, Santa Fe, New Mexico
1990	Cortland Jessup Gallery, Provincetown, Massachusetts
1989	Kauffman Gallery, Houston, Texas
1985	Soho 20 Gallery, New York, New York
1984	Elaine Starkman Gallery, New York, New York
	Blue Heron Gallery, Wellfleet, Massachusetts
1983	Soho 20 Gallery, New York, New York
	80 Washington Square East Galleries, New York, New York
1980	Noho Gallery, New York, New York
1977	Bethel Gallery, Bethel, Connecticut
1975	Katonah Gallery, Katonah, New York
1972	Silvermine Guild, New Canaan, Connecticut
1970	Gallery III, Ossining, New York
1969	Gallery III, Ossining, New York
1968	Briarcliff College, Briarcliff Manor, New York

Selected Group Exhibitions

2006	*Mergers and Acquisitions: recent additions to the permanent collection*, Museum of Fine Arts, Santa Fe, New Mexico
	Interlude, Charlotte Jackson Fine Art, Santa Fe, New Mexico
	Synthesis, Lemmons Contemporary, New York, New York
2005	*Natural Selection*, Charlotte Jackson Fine Art, Santa Fe, New Mexico
2004	*The Zen of Materiality*, trio exhibit, Charlotte Jackson Fine Art, Santa Fe, New Mexico

Selected Group Exhibitions, continued

2004 *Together*, Japan Art Forum, Kyoto, Japan

2003 *Explorations*, Charlotte Jackson Fine Art, Santa Fe, New Mexico

1999 *New Mexico 2000*, juried exhibition, Museum of Fine Arts, Santa Fe, New Mexico

Landscape: A Glimpse, Museum of Fine Arts, Santa Fe, New Mexico

1997 *Invitational*, Galerie Ulrike Buschlinger, Wiesbaden, Germany

House Guests, Linda Durham Contemporary Art, Galisteo, New Mexico

1996 *Archeology of the Spirit*, Gallery Brocken, Tokyo, Japan

Small Works – Group Show, Cortland Jessup Gallery, Provincetown, Massachusetts

1995 *The Landscape: New Mexico and Beyond*, Karan Ruhlen Gallery, Santa Fe, New Mexico

1994 *Our Own Visions: Abiquiu After O'Keeffe*,1994 Invitational Exhibit, Roswell Museum and Art Center, Roswell, New Mexico (catalogue)

Mnemonic Conflux, trio exhibit, Cast Iron Gallery, New York, New York (catalogue)

1993 *Summer Salon '93*, Spirit Gallery, Santa Fe, New Mexico

Invitational Shrine Show, Owings-Dewey Fine Art, Santa Fe, New Mexico

1992 *Abiquiu After O'Keeffe*, Galleria Arriba, Abiquiu, New Mexico

Inaugural Exhibition, Sally Harvey Fine Arts, Aspen, Colorado

1991 *A Sense of Place*, Peyton-Wright Galleries, Santa Fe, New Mexico (catalogue)

Selections '91, juried, College of Santa Fe, Santa Fe, New Mexico

A Salute to Women, National Museum of Women in the Arts, Washington, DC

1989 *In Quiet Contemplation*, Spirit Arts, Santa Fe, New Mexico

1988 *The Recovery Show*, Armory for the Arts, Santa Fe, New Mexico

1987 *Gallery Artists*, Enthios Gallery, Santa Fe, New Mexico

1986 *The Artist and the Spiritual Quest*, The Open Center, New York, New York

1985 *Private Vision*, Silvermine Guild, New Canaan, Connecticut

Member Artists '85, Katonah Gallery, Katonah, New York

1984 *Small Works*, Elaine Starkman Gallery, New York, New York

Member Artists, Soho 20 Gallery, New York, New York

	Silvermine Collection '84, Richardson-Vicks, Wilton, Connecticut
1983	*Collector's Choice*, curated by Ethel Scull, Pleiades Gallery, New York, New York
	Color Harmonious & Discordant, curated by Sylvia Sleigh, Marymount-Manhattan College, New York, New York
	Gallery Artists, Saugatuck Gallery, Westport, Connecticut
1982	*Member Artists*, Noho Gallery, New York, New York
1981	*The Advocate Show*, Hibbs Gallery, New York, New York
	Heresies Benefit Exhibition, Grey Art Gallery, New York, New York
	Annual Exhibition, juried, Provincetown Art Association, Provincetown, Massachusetts
1980	*International Festival of Women Artists*, Gallery 14, Copenhagen, Denmark
1978	*Southern New England Invitational*, Fairfield University, Fairfield, Connecticut
1976	*Members Exhibit*, Silvermine Guild, New Canaan, Connecticut
1975	*Invitational Exhibition*, Wooster Art Center, Wooster, Connecticut
	Juried Exhibition '75, juried by Dore Ashton and Richard Pousette-Dart, Rockland Center for the Arts, Rockland, New York
1973	*Group Exhibit*, Gallery One and Two, Hillside, New Jersey
1972	*New England Exhibition*, juried by Evan H. Turner, Silvermine Guild, New Canaan, Connecticut
1971	*New England Exhibition*, juried by Lawrence Alloway, Silvermine Guild, New Canaan, Connecticut
	Members Exhibition, Painting Award, WAS Gallery, Westchester Arts Society Gallery, Tarrytown, New York
1970	*New England Exhibition*, juried by Gordon M. Smith, Silvermine Guild, New Canaan, Connecticut
1969	*Faculty Exhibit*, Briarcliff College, Briarcliff Manor, New York
1968	*Faculty Exhibit*, State University of New York at New Paltz, New Paltz, New York
1967	*Members Exhibition*, Gallery of the Hawaii Arts Council, Honolulu, Hawaii
	MFA Exhibition, East West Center, University of Hawaii, Honolulu, Hawaii
1965	*Group Exhibit*, Honolulu Printmakers, Honolulu, Hawaii (traveling)
	Artists of Hawaii 1965, juried by Donald J. Brewer, Honolulu Academy of Arts, Honolulu, Hawaii

Selected Collections

Albright-Knox Art Gallery, Buffalo, New York

New Mexico Museum of Art, Santa Fe, New Mexico

The Harwood Foundation, Taos, New Mexico

Roswell Museum and Art Center, Roswell, New Mexico

Upaya Foundation, Santa Fe, New Mexico

Cravath, Swain & Moore, New York, New York

Hubert Wilke, Inc., New York, New York

Babkie International, Westport, Connecticut

Barnard College, New York, New York

Marilyn Rubin Associates, Briarcliff Manor, New York

Sandek Corporation, Stanford, Connecticut

Collins & Aikman Corporation, New York, New York

Library and Research Center, National Museum of Women in the Arts, Washington, DC

Bowes and Associates, Houston, Texas

Robert Redford, Santa Monica, California

Selected Bibliography

Center for Contemporary Art, "Talk on Light," by Joan Watts, July 2005; illus.

Artists of the Southwest, by Douglas Bullis, 2004; illus.

The New Mexican, "Nothing added or taken away," by Denise Kusel, July 2000; illus.

The New Mexican, "Joan Watts: The Light Radiates from Within," by Dottie Indyke, Sept. 1998; illus.

Joan Watts, catalogue, Galerie Ulrike Buschlinger, essay by Jan Adlmann, 1997; illus.

Wiesbaden Kurier and *Weisbaden Tagblatt*, July 1996; illus.

The New Mexican, "Watts' Studio Provides an Art Alternative," by Lis Bensley, Oct. 1995; illus.

Our Own Visions: Abiquiu After O'Keeffe, exhibition catalogue, by Wesley Rusnell, Sept. 1994; illus.

THE, "Joan Watts-Black/White: Paintings," by Christine Hemp, Aug. 1994; illus.

The New Mexican, "Abstractions Stripped to the Bone," by Lis Bensley, July 1994

Mnemonic Conflux, exhibition catalogue, essay by Martha Scott, Feb. 1994; illus.
THE, "Critical Reflections," by Diane Armitage, Oct. 1993; illus.
The New Mexican, "Gallery Hopping," by Dean Balsamo, Sept. 1993.
The New Mexican, "A Sense of Place," by Pancho Epstein, Nov. 1991; illus.
Albuquerque Journal, "Back to the Land," by David Steinberg, Nov. 1991; illus.
Art News, "New York Review," by Eleanor Heartney, Feb. 1984; illus.
Women Artists News, "Sexism and Ageism in the World," by Margaret Gosden, Nov. 1984; illus.
Art News, "The Artist's Artist," by Grace Gluck, Nov. 1982; illus.
Village Voice, "ART," by Carrie Rickey, Sept 3–9, 1980.
Women Artists News, "An International Sampling of the Visual Arts," by Janice Willard, Oct. 1980.
New York Arts Journal, "Gallery Reviews," by Leslie Plummer, Nov. 1980.
Artspeak, "The Circles of Joan Watts," by Palmer Peroner, Nov. 1980; illus.
Bridgeport Sunday Post, "Joan Watts–Tondo Paintings," by Martha Scott, Feb. 1977; illus.
Patent Trader, "Outposts of Art," by Noel Frackman, Jan. 1970.

Education

1964–1966 University of Hawaii, M.F.A.
1960–1963 San Francisco Art Institute, B.F.A.
1957–1959 Briarcliff College, A.A.S.

Teaching Positions

1968–1977 Briarcliff College, Associate Professor
1966–1968 State University of New York at New Paltz, Assistant Professor
1964–1966 University of Hawaii, Instructor

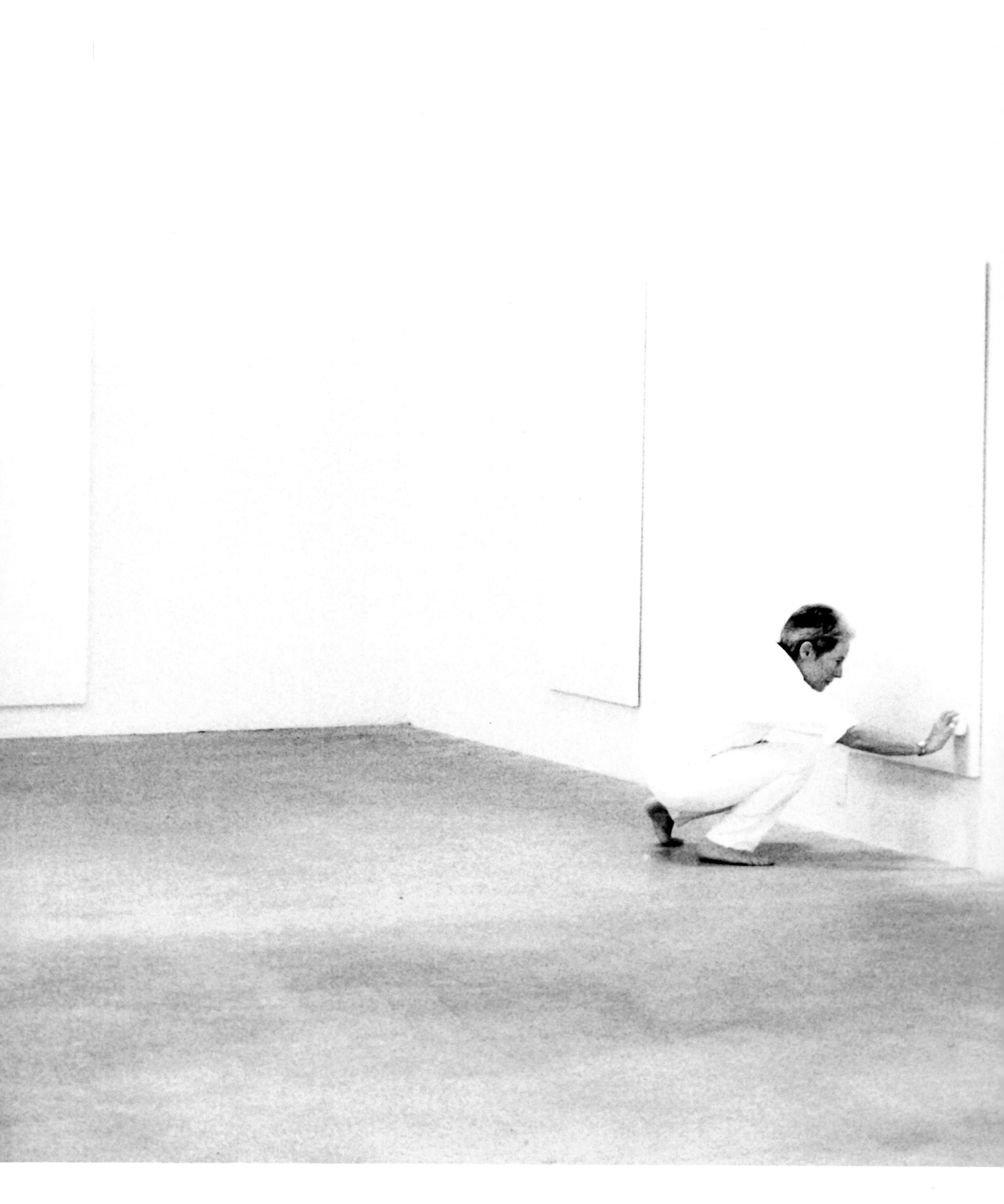

Acknowledgments

left: Watts in her studio, 2000
photo: Erika Blumenfeld

The path of painting is not a journey taken alone. Others have given me necessary support for which I am deeply grateful.

Richard Berman's impeccable craftsmanship provides the physical support for my work.

Herbert Lotz photographs my paintings with a perfect eye for the subtle light required.

David Chickey designed a beautiful catalogue for *Series Zero* and he has created this book which is its own work of art.

Lilly Wei's text has deeply penetrated the evolving story of my painting, skillfully translating my vision into exquisite language.

Louis Grachos has written an insightful foreword and has given affirmation to my work by including it in the collection of the Albright-Knox.

Bobbie Lemmons has truly made this book possible. She believed in the project and paved the way. She and Charlotte Jackson are bringing my work out of the studio and into the world.

I am indebted to each for their skills and creativity in supporting my painting process and bringing this book into being, and I am honored by Radius Books for their stunning publication of my life's work.

This first printing of JOAN WATTS is limited to 1000 copies. The book was set in Din, and printed on 176gsm McCoy matte paper. All artwork copyright ©2008 Joan Watts. Designed by Skolkin+Chickey, Santa Fe, NM. Edited by David Chickey and Darius Himes. Proofread by Laura Addison.

RADIUS BOOKS is a tax exempt 501 (c)(3) nonprofit organization, founded in 2007, whose mission is to encourage, promote, and publish books of artistic and cultural value.

Books give an accessible form to rich and complex creative visions. They become the vehicles for beauty, reflection, and change. In this spirit, RADIUS BOOKS donates copies of every title it publishes to libraries and schools—with the hope and expectation that these books will reach new and expanding audiences.

To learn more about the mission of RADIUS BOOKS, please visit www.radiusbooks.org.

RADIUS BOOKS 1012 Marquez Place, #109B Santa Fe, NM 87505 www.radiusbooks.org
Founding publishers: David Chickey, Darius Himes, Joanna Hurley, & David Skolkin

Available through D.A.P. / DISTRIBUTED ART PUBLISHERS
155 Sixth Ave. 2nd Floor, New York, NY 10013 t: (212) 627-1999

ISBN-10: 1-934435-05-8 ISBN-13: 978-1-934435-05-2
Library of Congress Cataloguing-in-Publication Data available on request

Printed and bound in Phoenix, AZ

IMAGES:
Page 2: Artist's Studio, 2008
Page 5: Installation View, Lemmons Contemporary, New York, New York, 2007, photo: Roberto Portillo
Pages 6 & 7: *0-36*, 2003
Page 8: Installation View, Artist's Studio, 2007
All installation photos by Herb Lotz unless otherwise noted.